"*During my forty years in business, I've hired thousands. If you want a job, want to keep it and advance, read this book!*"

—William S. Lee
Chairman Emeritus
Duke Power Company

"*I warmly commend Tony Zeiss's book,* The 12 Essential Laws for Getting a Job . . . and Becoming Indispensable. *It is readable, full of practical wisdom and inspiration, and an excellent guide book for almost anyone looking for a job. Most of all, it shines with the spirit of the author whose caring heart, experience, and personal achievement model what he writes about.*"

—Dr. Leighton Ford
Leighton Ford Ministries

"*Getting and keeping a good job is a universal concern today. This book provides timely and practical solutions to this problem. Based on many years of employing and evaluating job performance, I highly recommend the excellent advice of this expertly written book.*"

—Ray Killian
Executive Vice President
Belk Stores, Inc.

"*In an era of increasing job insecurity, this book is essential reading for everyone. The effects of downsizing and growing competition will ripple through the economy for years, and so all of us must be prepared to search out new career opportunities.* The 12 Essential Laws for Getting a Job . . . and Becoming Indispensable *provides the guidance and the tools needed to succeed in this search.*"

—David R. Pierce
President
American Association of
Community Colleges

"Dr. Zeiss has reduced the complex task of getting a good job into a simple, straightforward formula for success. His positive and easy-to-read style makes this book an indispensable tool for job seekers throughout America!" —Zig Ziglar
Chairman of the Board
The Zig Ziglar Corporation

"The 12 Essential Laws for Getting a Job . . . and Becoming Indispensable *is entertaining as well as educational—a must read."*
—John M. Lovorn, Jr.
President and CEO
The Pace Group

"In this era of fast-paced change in corporate America, replete with downsizings, changing skill sets, and global competition, this book offers a refreshing and much-needed how-to approach to finding, keeping, and advancing one's employment. The 12 Essential Laws for Getting a Job . . . and Becoming Indispensable *is an indispensable source of proven methodologies, skills, and attitudes about working successfully in the U.S."*
—James R. Bavis
Vice President of Corporate
Employee Relations
Sprint

"The text provides practical and workable tips for those in the job market for the first time as well as for those experienced individuals making a change of career later in life."
—Eugene L. Hartwig
Senior Vice President
Kelly Services

"A positive attitude is indeed the key to any successful venture. Tony Zeiss's book conveys practical, upbeat ideas and

suggestions for the unemployed or underutilized employee. This book is a perfect road map for anyone pursuing employment or self-improvement. Zeiss's practical advice will give a boost to anyone's career aspirations, as well as useful pointers on how to successfully approach the daunting search for a new job."

—Parris N. Glendening
Governor
State of Maryland

"This book successfully presents the work ethics and skills today's Americans need for getting and keeping jobs. It's an easy-to-read career resource that will help all workers."

—Representative Sue Myrick

"As a long-term retailer, I've employed thousands of people over the years. The most successful practiced the very behaviors presented in the laws outlined in this book. Every job seeker and worker should read it!"

—John M. Belk
Chairman of the Board
Belk Stores Services, Inc.

"In a world where we all face not just loss of a single job but full career change, help is always welcome. When the help actually has a chance of working, there is real value. The 12 Essential Laws for Getting a Job . . . and Becoming Indispensable *fits into that category."*

—Lynn Martin
Former Secretary of the
U.S. Department of Labor

THE 12 ESSENTIAL LAWS FOR

GETTING A JOB...

AND BECOMING INDISPENSABLE

DR. TONY ZEISS

THOMAS NELSON PUBLISHERS
Nashville • Atlanta • London • Vancouver

Published in Nashville, Tennessee, by Thomas Nelson, Inc., Publishers, and distributed in Canada by Word Communications, Ltd., Richmond, British Columbia.

The Bible version used in this publication is THE NEW KING JAMES VERSION. Copyright © 1979, 1980, 1982, Thomas Nelson, Inc., Publishers.

Library of Congress Cataloging-in-Publication Data

Zeiss, Anthony.
 The 12 essential laws for getting a job—and becoming indispensable / Tony Zeiss.
  p. cm.
  ISBN 0-7852-7564-9 (pbk.)
  1. Vocational guidance. I. Title.
HF5381.Z33 1997
650.14—dc20   96–36580
                CIP

Printed in the United States of America.
1 2 3 4 5 6 — 02 01 00 99 98 97

CONTENTS

FOREWORD

Few activities are more important in life than finding and keeping a job. My observations while traveling throughout the world as a business consultant suggest that the sense of worth and self-esteem that comes through work is universally pervasive, whether in the oil fields of the Middle East or the towers of Manhattan.

Yet finding these self-fulfilling opportunities is becoming more and more difficult regardless of location. Millions of Americans are out of work. In Europe, unemployment stands at an uncomfortably high rate of 10 to 15 percent. Elsewhere the problem is more precarious. According to various estimates, one-third of the world's population is either unemployed or underemployed. That's about two billion grumbling souls.

Within the United States, continual downsizing and outsourcing, coupled with mergers, acquisitions, and relocations, have placed many people in the job market in recent years. And there is little reason to suppose that this trend will be any different in the future.

It is absolutely imperative that everyone of working age understands, expects, and prepares to be between jobs, or transitional, at some time in a working career. How people respond to this virtually assured eventuality will determine the speed and success that they can expect in identifying and landing the fulfilling work opportunity that awaits them.

Many books have been written, and numerous courses have been developed, regarding the technical aspects of job seeking. Information on such tasks as resume writing, skills inventorying, company identification, and job search techniques is readily available. However, books or courses on preparing oneself emotionally and psychologically for the job search and the next job are scarce. And the ones that are available tend to focus on highly sophisticated and pedantic approaches that few job seekers with less than a Ph.D. in psychology will understand, let alone try to emulate.

That is precisely why a book like this one is so vital to transitional workers. It helps them to understand and develop personal characteristics that will be necessary for the job searches that will surely lie ahead of them at some point.

As a consultant for thirty years to hundreds of America's large, medium, and small companies, I can attest that *The 12 Essential Laws for Getting a Job . . . and Becoming Indispensable* is dead on target. Transitional workers who read this book and use the principles outlined by Dr. Zeiss will definitely have an advantage for landing good jobs and keeping them. Just as corporate America is changing in order to be globally competitive, America's workers must also change. The information in this powerful, yet easy to read, book will help them to make the life adjustments for successful and satisfying careers.

The twelve essential laws discussed in this book represent the top twelve characteristics that employers most want in employees. What might be surprising to many readers is that ten of the twelve relate to personal characteristics and only two relate to educational qualifications and work experience.

Not long ago I met with the vice president of human resources for a major railroad. She had just finished interviewing a job applicant for an important position within the company. As this longtime business associate of mine met me in the company reception area, I sensed she was despondent. She was, and without any prompting, she said she had just finished an interview with a job applicant who looked "perfect on paper" but turned out to be "pathetic on personality." She went on to say that the company requires self-starters, people who can function comfortably in a team environment.

Senior officers of many small and large companies throughout the world have expressed these same concerns to me in recent years—this at a time when more and more companies are pushing more and more responsibility to the workers in the office cubicle and on the factory floor, when middle management and formal manufacturing structures have all but disappeared. What they look for, and desperately need, in new employees are the traits outlined so knowingly in this book. Such personal characteristics as being a good listener, having a strong work ethic, and reflecting a positive attitude are at the top of the employer's list of job candidate attributes.

If someone really and truly wants a job, and is really and truly committed to living up to God's potential, this book will help that person find the way to self-esteem, self-reliance, and self-satisfaction through meaningful and rewarding work.

Robert M. Ady
Deloitte & Touche/Fantus Consulting

PREFACE

You can achieve these twelve essential laws for getting a job. The sooner you learn them and use them, the sooner you will find the employment you seek. Further, using these same laws at work will help you in job advancement and will provide the best job security possible. But first, a word of warning. You will not be successful using these laws to get or advance in a job unless you are emotionally prepared to take them and use them seriously and consistently.

Most unemployed and underemployed workers feel rejected, defeated, cheated, or perplexed. They usually go through an emotional process similar to the stages of grief, that is, denial, followed by anger, depression, fear, sometimes guilt, and finally acceptance. These changing emotions are quite normal. Unfortunately, emotions and innermost feelings drive beliefs and shape self-concept. In consequence, what you feel, you believe. And belief drives behavior. If you are depressed or angry when you have a job interview or when you network for job leads, your speech, your posture, and all of your nonverbal actions telegraph that depression or anger. That is why you have to work through any negative feelings surrounding your current employment condition and get on with the positive and successful adventure of landing a new job!

Yes, searching for a new or better job is an adventure. It is much like buying an automobile. If you try to pick out a new car without any preparation, you will likely be disappointed. In fact, there is a good chance a salesperson will make most of your car selection decisions for you. But with the proper attitude and planning, you will likely get the vehicle you have dreamed of at an affordable price. You will enjoy the car-seeking process because of the comfort that comes from first knowing what you want, what you can afford, and how you will negotiate with the dealer. When you are finished, you will have grown in knowledge and skills from the entire process, and your confidence in purchasing automobiles will remain forever better.

With proper planning and a positive attitude, you can make your job search just as much of an adventure as buying an automobile, and your confidence in getting good jobs in the future will increase dramatically.

You can use scores of resources to assist in your job search. Employment agencies, outplacement firms, temporary agencies, and worker leasing agencies can all be effective, but they generally charge a fee for their services. Public libraries, school and college libraries, community colleges, small business development centers, and World Wide Web computer networks can be valuable. But it is up to you—and only you—to sell yourself. The twelve essential laws presented in this book will guide you in selling yourself successfully to an employer.

You can use any number of gimmicks to give yourself an edge in the job-seeking process. Sending your applications by overnight mail, printing business cards with your career objective prominently displayed, and printing professional resumes can help in the success-ful acquisition of employment, but using the twelve laws described in this book will be significantly more effective. Ignore any of them and all the gimmicks in the world will not help. Each law is unique. Learn them, live them, and use them to your advantage.

These twelve laws present the primary traits em-ployers want in employees. The top ten laws are attitu-dinal in nature. That is, you can make them a part of your life by believing in them and deciding to use them. You see, positive behavior is essential to career success. The remaining two laws emphasize work preparation and prior experience.

The formula for a successful job-hunting experience is this: (1) believe in yourself, (2) focus on your job goal, and (3) employ the twelve essential laws for get-ting a job!

Acknowledgments

Many thanks to my wife, Beth,
to Wendy Stone, and to
the four people who helped
in the reviewing of
this book:

Lindsay Allen, President
Mark III Personnel

Bob Baxter, Vice President/Partner
Korn/Ferry International

John Garcia,
Professional Speaker
and Management Consultant

Jim Bavis, Vice President
Sprint

INTRODUCTION

Every day millions of Americans seeking employment misspend countless hours and dollars. If they only knew the secrets to successful employment, they could save the wasted hours and dollars they are spending on marginally effective job-seeking techniques and move straight to employment success. Research describing the specific attributes employers seek has been available for years, but few people pay any attention to it. Instead, millions of job seekers continue to focus on developing the wrong skills.

Too many job seekers blindly accept the advice presented by well-meaning resume writers, career psychologists, and job acquisition experts as the best way to land a new job. They are often misled. Nonetheless, job seekers thrust all their energies into developing power resumes, practicing clever interviewing skills, and learning to network. Although these things are significant, they do very little to help job seekers recognize the traits employers seek.

Further, too many job seekers develop the misconception that they are inadequate, underskilled, or discriminated against because of age, race, gender, size, or any number of self-created excuses to protect their fragile egos. This is typical, but self-defeating, behavior. Regardless of your situation, you can and must emphasize your strengths and have the confidence to sell yourself in the job market.

As the United States shifts into a global economy, its businesses are moving into a perpetual state of rightsizing. That is, they downsize to become more competitive and upsize as demands for their new products and services increase. Corporate America, and in some cases the public sector, is reengineering to increase its competitive stature by focusing on more efficient processes, greater productivity, and reduced labor costs. In short, America's private and public employers are undergoing a continuous process of job elimination and job creation as a necessary competitive technique. This is a natural process. Consider jobs in agriculture. In 1900, 95 percent of the workforce was in agriculture. Today, less than 2 percent of the workforce is employed in this area. The average worker today will change jobs seven times and change careers three times during his or her working years. America's workers need to become more entrepreneurial and view themselves as enterprises, commodities to be marketed.

To survive in this new work environment, workers must understand how to best prepare themselves and sell themselves in the open job market. They can do this by developing a clear career goal and by undertaking and practicing the traits employers most seek in their employees. Successful career professionals know how to leave the past behind them and look ever forward to their goal. They know that the best predictor of success is to have a clear goal and the self-discipline to continuously work toward it.

After twenty-eight years of helping people with job training and job acquisition skills, I have fleshed out the twelve attributes that employers most prefer among potential and existing employees. As a state job training council chair, college president, and chair of the National Workforce Development Commission for the American Association of Community Colleges, I can attest that these twelve personal traits make all the difference between a successful and an unsuccessful job search.

I call these job acquisition attributes the twelve essential laws for getting a job. By learning and using these laws in your search for a new job (or keeping the one you have), you dramatically increase your chances for success.

CHAPTER 1

DOUBLE A'S

———❦———

*All the days of the afflicted are evil,
But he who is of a merry heart has a
continual feast.*

—Proverb

THE FIRST AND MOST IMPORTANT
LAW FOR GETTING A GOOD JOB
IS HAVING ALTITUDE IN
YOUR ATTITUDE!

The most important attribute for landing a great job is a positive attitude. And guess who has absolute control over your attitude? You are correct! You alone determine how you will face each day, react to each circumstance, and behave toward others. People, especially employers, want to be associated with positive people, happy people.

You can verify the truth of this successful job-seeking trait by asking yourself these questions:

- Do I most enjoy positive or negative people at social events?
- Do I most enjoy being around positive or negative people at work?
- Do I think positive or negative people most often reach their goals?

The answers are obvious. You would much rather be associated with optimistic, cheerful people, especially during work.

Employer research indicates that a positive attitude is nearly always at the very top of the list of desirable characteristics for employees. It's no wonder, then, that the most successful job applicants have a positive attitude.

I can cite scores of examples of people who lost jobs or could not find jobs because of their poor attitudes. These people seem to relish their chronic discontent, and then they complain when employers dismiss them or refuse to hire them. One good illustration, however, comes from my experience as a fifteen-year-old. Along with many of my friends, I took a job detasseling seed corn one summer in central Indiana. We stood for eight hours a day in metal cages that hung off both sides of an elevated tractor. After a few days of the heat, dust, corn poison, and a humorless tobacco-spitting boss, I became discontented and voiced my grievances loudly and often to anyone who would listen. Predictably, the boss and I parted company with mutual satisfaction. It took a while, about two weeks of being home without my friends who continued to work, but I finally realized that the problem was mine and I'd better learn from the experience. It became clear that I'd never be happy in any job unless I changed my attitude about work.

Anxiety as an Ally

The key to a successful job search is to develop and maintain a success-oriented attitude from the very beginning. Overcoming self-doubt, anger, bitterness, and other self-defeating attitudes is often the greatest challenge for workers in transition. As John Belk of Belk Department Stores often advises, "Whining about your problems to others is a waste of time; half of them don't care and the other half are glad you've got them." This is an overstatement, of course, but the point is well made.

Whether you are looking for your first job or your twentieth job, you have reason to feel some anxiety. But you can leverage the anxiety into a powerful ally to be successful. You see, a little anxiety keeps you mentally alert and drives you into action. And guess what? You're not alone out there in the job-seeking market. The U.S. Department of Labor reports that 5.7 percent of the employment population or nearly fourteen million workers are in transition today in these United States! You see, people are changing jobs as employment demands change and as they pursue their career goals. The good news is that we're in the middle of an expanding economy, and millions of new jobs are being created every decade in our great country. The better news is that virtually all fourteen million of America's transitional workers will find a good job if they keep a positive attitude, gain the appropriate skills, and remain persistent. As a matter of fact, U.S. government statistics indicate that approximately 22 percent of American workers, nearly 30 million people, find new employment each year. This means 2.5 million people find new employment each month, 625,000 each week, and 125,000 each day. With the proper attitude, the odds of getting new employment are very good. Remember, you are not unemployed; you're simply a worker in transition as everyone is at some time in life.

But life's been unfair to me, you may be thinking. Welcome to the club! Life is full of unfairness, unhappiness, and negativism. We can clamor all we want about the unfairness of life's circumstances, but absolutely nothing will change those circumstances unless we resolve to change them through conscious action. At this point in your life you may not feel in control. But you'll always have the option to be in control of one thing—your attitude. You see, it's not what happens *to* you that matters; it's what happens *in* you that matters. By controlling your attitude, in a certain sense you control your destiny.

Working in an atmosphere of low morale is always difficult. Unfortunately, too many people choose to believe their morale is determined by their supervisors or by other workers. In truth, people should not allow their morale to be determined by anyone except themselves. Mature, successful people choose to be responsible for their morale, regardless of their circumstances.

Facing the Day

Only one person can decide how you will face each day. The temptation to seek safety, to avoid taking risks, to give up on dreams is forever around you. But positive people know how to keep faith in themselves and in their abilities. You can control your thoughts, and your thoughts control your emotions and attitudes. If you don't like the facts, you can change your attitudes about them. It takes some practice, but millions of people do it every day. By looking at any situation from a detached viewpoint, you can begin to see different, even positive, dimensions of the situation. How many times have you worried yourself sick over something that never materialized? Or more likely, how many times have you experienced something terribly negative in your life only to see it as a positive growth experience in retrospect?

One technique that often helps to reduce excess anxiety or worry is to ask yourself the following questions when you are faced with a major problem:

- Does it threaten my soul?
- Does it threaten my family?
- Does it threaten my life?
- How important will this be fifty or one hundred years from now?

This exercise helps you get in control of your thoughts about your transitional (temporary) employment condition by developing the proper perspective. Once you can control your thoughts, you can eliminate negative thinking and replace it with a positive, success-oriented attitude. You become positive simply by thinking positively!

Positive Examples

Successful job seekers and job keepers are noted for their persistent optimism and infectious cheerfulness. They are fun to be around because they are so encouraging. Take Dick Vitale, for instance. If you mention the name Dick Vitale practically anywhere in America, he will be immediately identified as that "supercharged college basketball announcer." It is safe to state that Vitale is one of the most enthusiastic people in the world today. Was he always as famous and successful as he is today? Absolutely not. Just like everyone else, Dick Vitale worked hard, paid his professional dues, and struggled to balance career and family responsibilities. Did he have it much different from other people who grew up in his neighborhood? Certainly not. But he possessed one thing that propelled him to the success he and his family enjoy today: a positive attitude.

I sat next to Dick Vitale on an airplane bound for Raleigh, North Carolina. He'd had little sleep, but he was flying to his next game with enthusiasm. His eyes sparkled when we talked about some of the Detroit Pistons he used to coach, but they really brightened when he spoke about his family. He also told me that he was about to appear in his fifth movie and that he had become a best-selling author. It was clear he loved his work and his family. As the plane began its descent to land, I asked him what personal attributes most contributed to his success. Without hesitation he replied, "Passion, enthusiasm, and a positive attitude for what I do." There you have it. Staying motivated, enthusiastic, and optimistic is a strong formula for career success and accomplished living. And you don't have to look very far to find other examples of successful people who recognized the law of an elevated attitude.

Dave Thomas of Wendy's fame, for example, had to overcome some tremendous adversities before he became successful. He was an orphan, failed to finish high school, and washed dishes for a living. But he had one survival instinct that helped him rise to the top in the competitive fast-food business: a positive attitude.

Look at Muggsy Bogues, the famous NBA point guard who stands only five feet three inches tall. Or Alonzo Mourning, the orphan who has become one of the NBA's great centers in recent years. How about Sandra Day O'Connor, who broke the gender barrier on the U.S. Supreme Court? Having observed these successful people in the media, I believe their optimistic and self-reliant attitudes propelled them into greatness. The point is obvious. If you want to be successful at landing a great job and having a rewarding, successful career, be positive.

Conclusion

Successful job seekers almost always have a clear career goal in mind, they have faith in themselves, and they jump into the job search process with relish. They make up their minds to view the job search process as an adventure, and they see themselves as a desirable product or service to be marketed. Most of all, they have an unquenchable spirit of optimism and cheerfulness, and they know that the impressions they make on others are important, especially the first one. A constant review of the altitude of the attitude is essential for all successful job seekers. This law of attitude will contribute to your job-acquisition and job-keeping skills more than any other law reviewed in this book.

Practical Advice

Remember that employers value and seek employees with good attitudes. Make up your mind right now to concentrate on your blessings and your strengths, not your troubles. Make a conscious decision to be cheerful and optimistic. As Vince Lombardi used to say, "If you're not fired with enthusiasm, you'll be fired with enthusiasm." Demonstrate your positive attitude by practicing it in every situation and in everything you do—in conversation, job research, resume writing, letters of application, and non-job-search-related activities. Try to focus all of your attention on the person or persons with whom you're talking. You especially need to be positive during all direct contacts with anyone who can potentially help you get a job.

You must learn to control your attitude by thinking positively in all situations and at all times so that you, in fact, become positive. The first few seconds of your job interview are most important. Your broad smile, confident posture, firm handshake, and sincere greeting are essential in making a good impression. I've interviewed thousands of people and assisted thousands more who sought employment, and I can tell you unequivocally that my impression of them was always determined within the first minute or so of our meeting each other. Yes, sometimes that initial impression changed over time, but first impressions die hard, and most job seekers never get a second chance to change that impression. Frankly, if I don't see excitement in the eye, cheerfulness in the heart, and a genuine positive nature within the applicant, I move to the next finalist. The lesson? Make that first impression a great one by having an uplifting, enthusiastic, and consistently positive attitude!

POINTS TO PONDER

1. You are not alone.
2. Stay positive.
3. Good jobs are out there.
4. Keep the faith.
5. Make it an adventure.
6. Impressions are lasting.

FROM THIS DAY FORWARD

(This section, which will appear at the end of each chapter, is designed to help you internalize and apply each law in your daily life.)

1. Example: "I will be cheerful, enthusiastic, and grateful for my blessings."
2. Example: "I will not participate in whining, criticizing, or demeaning others."
3. Example: "I will view my job search as an adventure!"
4. _____.

CHAPTER 2

THE CAPITAL C

———

Once a human being has arrived on this earth, communication is the largest single factor determining what kinds of relationships he makes with others and what happens to him in the world about him.

—Virginia Satir

THE SECOND MOST IMPORTANT LAW FOR GETTING A GOOD JOB IS BEING AN EFFECTIVE COMMUNICATOR!

Most job seekers think that technical skills and prior experience are the most important determinants for getting a job in today's sophisticated workplace. They are wrong. Survey after survey of America's employers indicates that the most successful job applicants are those who can communicate well. In fact, my research indicates that the possession of specific technical skills and prior experience rank as the lowest two laws for getting a job. Of course, they are necessary, but there are ten laws before them that you should recognize as being critical to your future employment.

All the knowledge and technical skills known to humanity are useless to an employer unless you can communicate to other people. If you have good technical skills and experience in a career field, but you have problems getting or keeping a job, the chances are high that you have violated the second law of getting a job.

The capital C law underscores the critical dimension of communication. People judge us in large measure by the way we communicate. Unfair as it may sound, the truth is, people evaluate us by the way they see and hear us. Everyone communicates, but not everyone communicates effectively. The law of communicating to get a job emphasizes the need to (1) make a good impression, (2) project confidence, and (3) build trusting relationships quickly. People who become effective at using the law of communication in this respect will have few problems becoming employed in their chosen career field.

You can demonstrate the truth of this law by answering the following questions:

- How many really good communicators have I known who were out of work very long?

- If I had my choice to spend a social evening with a good communicator or a poor communicator, which one would I select?
- If an employer has the choice (and he or she usually has) of hiring a good communicator or a poor one, which applicant do I think will get the job?

The ability to make effective group presentations is becoming increasingly important in the world of work, but this law of communication mostly involves basic interpersonal communication skills. Verbal skills, non-verbal skills, and writing skills are of particular relevance to transitional workers. I have interviewed hundreds of job applicants who have had impeccable credentials and impressive resumes, but their interviews, body language, and/or cover letters cost them any chance of serious consideration.

The Interviewer

Just put yourself in the place of the employer for a moment. As the person doing the hiring or the recommending for hiring, your credibility and judgment are on the line. The next promotion may well depend on your ability to employ productive people. If you are the owner of a company, your ability to search out the best employees among many applicants becomes even more essential. The very existence of your business may depend on it.

Now let's assume you are screening all applicants for a position and must narrow them to three finalists to be interviewed. Chances are good that you will first measure the applicants' minimum qualifications for the job. Beyond that, your intuition, based on the input available on the application materials, is all you have to screen them to the top three finalists. What would you look at to make your selection process easier? You would probably look for applicants who had the best qualifications, the most experience, the greatest stability, and the best reference letters. Next, you would look at their cover letters closely to glean any additional information that might help you decide to keep or reject the applicant. If a cover letter is messy, is full of grammatical glitches, and generally does not communicate, what will you do? You will pitch it. After all, your task at this point is to select the top three applicants from among many. You will use anything that can disqualify them in your mind. And it does not matter how good the qualifications and prior experience looked; if they submitted a sloppy cover letter, they will most likely be sloppy in their work.

Pretend you have selected your three finalists and have set up interviews. The primary purpose of the interview is to help you employ the best person for the position. This is your opportunity to meet the candidates face-to-face. Ninety-nine times out of one hundred you will employ the finalist who makes the best impression during the interview. The interviewee who speaks with the most confidence, who listens best, and who has the best overall appearance and body language is the one you will employ. In short, employers are just like you. Once all things are mostly equal, they will hire the person they feel best about, the person they are impressed with the most. In every employment situation the objective process of checking qualifications, experience, and references eventually shifts to a subjective process of intuition, feeling, and general impressions. The applicant who has the best attitude and communication skills inevitably gets the job.

Employers clearly understand that people make or break their careers and their businesses. This recognition has caused employers to become experts at screening job applicants. Some of them use a sophisticated system for screening prospective employees while others simply review applications and resumes. In either case, however, the gut feeling they get from the interview or from prior association with the applicant really drives their decision to hire or not to hire. *But that's just not fair,* you might be thinking. Fair or not, when it's your job or your business that's at stake, the survival instinct is very strong, and interviewers, within the parameters of the law, will choose the person they think to be best for the position. The good news is that you can take advantage of the capital C law by learning to be a great communicator.

They Really Communicate!

Just what constitutes a good interpersonal communicator? Barbara Bush, our former First Lady, is one of the very best one-on-one communicators I have ever met. When she talks to you, she is completely focused on you and the conversation with every fiber of her being. Her eyes never divert from yours, her personal warmth envelops you, and she listens intently. Our eleven-year-old son summed up Mrs. Bush's communication expertise best after he first met her by stating, "She made me feel really important!" Mrs. Bush is certainly expert at (1) making a good impression, (2) projecting confidence, and (3) building trusting relationships quickly.

Not everyone has the skills of Barbara Bush, but everyone can learn to have them. Even people with basic communication disabilities can overcome them if motivated to do so. Think of Helen Keller. She lost her sight and hearing before she was two years old. She could not even speak. With dogged determination and the help of Anne Sullivan, Helen Keller graduated from Radcliffe with honors and eventually became internationally famous as an author, lecturer, and spokesperson for people with physical disabilities.

I once interviewed a finalist for a teaching position at a college where I was president. He had a painfully obvious speech disability, but he spoke with confidence, never once acknowledging or apologizing for his articulation disability. Further, he convinced me that his goal in life was to help others through teaching. It was clear he had the heart and the desire to be the best teacher in his field. I trusted him to put our customers (students) first. His competitors were far more articulate, but they seemed less committed. The applicant with the disability got the job and rapidly became one of the most respected and sought-after instructors in the entire college.

A final word about people with communication deficiencies is in order. Consider Moses. His brother Aaron spoke for him in many formal settings, yet Moses led his people out of bondage, remained their undisputed leader for forty years, and wrote several books of the Bible. The point is clear. You can use the capital C law to get the job of your dreams if you really want to, and you do not have to be perfect to be successful. If you have a deficiency in one communication area, you can often make up for it by emphasizing another.

Assess Yourself

Even if you do not think you have a deficiency in communicating, you would do well to assess your communication strengths and weaknesses. Often, your best friend or your spouse will be honest enough to point them out to you. In any event, attending a class or seminar on communication techniques is advisable. Brushing up on communication skills is always a good idea since these skills generally assist in all of life's endeavors. An assessment of your adeptness in the following areas will be most useful for your job search:

- Speech. Seek an honest critique of your ability to speak in casual and in formal settings. Employers especially value your skills at making presentations. Also, be sure your volume and intonation are adequate and your diction is good. Work at eliminating anything that distracts from your effectiveness when speaking.

- Body language. Believe it or not, your body language speaks volumes to the observer. Assess your posture in a variety of settings. Photographs and videotape recordings are especially revealing. Concentrate on holding eye contact, keeping pleasant facial expressions, and remaining poised in all circumstances.

- Writing. Get someone to review your writing skills, particularly as they apply to cover letters, resumes, and thank-you notes. Grammar checks and spell checks are nice on the computer, but they are no substitute for effective writing.

- Communication etiquette. Seek an honest assessment of your ability to listen well and to participate in social conversations. Do you encourage conversation by introducing topics and by asking questions of others? Do you stay focused on other people's thoughts or are your own more interesting to you?

- Paralanguage. The best conversationalist is an active listener. Does your paralanguage—verbal sounds of agreement, surprise, understanding, and disagreement, for example—encourage and compliment others when they're talking?

Many of these communication attributes come naturally to you. Others are not so natural, but you can learn them. However you choose to learn to communicate effectively, you must be able to gain people's confidence through sincerity. One technique for developing good communication skills is to emulate someone whom you think does well in this area. It could be a politician, a teacher, a salesperson, or anyone who has proven success in dealing with others on a consistent basis. Confidence comes from being prepared. After you have brushed up on your communication skills, anticipate every question regarding your job search and the job interview. (See chapter 9 for a sample list of interview questions.) After a short time, your answers will be spontaneous, and your sincerity will show.

Conclusion

Communicating effectively is an essential law for getting the job you want. It begins with planning and ends with making a great impression on paper and during the interview. Once you have chosen the job you most wish to get, plan for it and develop the confidence that you will be the best for that job. Making a good impression seldom happens by accident. The secret to making a good impression is to become as good as you would like to be. In other words, if you hope to present yourself to others as a positive person who is goal oriented with a strong work ethic, you should become such a person. Pretense is a heavy burden and is always discovered in the end. Just be sincere and be yourself—your best self—and you will increase your chances for getting the job of your dreams. Strive to become a good communicator and you'll be astonished at how easy it is to make a good impression, project confidence, and build trusting relationships.

Practical Advice

Remember that employers behave just as you would if you were in their place. They are looking for the best candidate for the available position. They do this through an objective screening process and through a subjective, impression-based process. Your attitude is extremely important, but your ability to communicate is also important. Make a conscious decision to assess your verbal and nonverbal communication skills, and resolve to improve by adopting techniques of successful people and by attending a communication class or seminar. Answering anticipated questions with sincerity and thought is essential during networking as well as during interviews. But you must not overlook making a good impression through facial expressions, posture, and listening skills. The lesson? Be prepared, be sincere, and communicate with confidence!

POINTS TO PONDER

1. Make a good impression.
2. Project confidence.
3. Build trusting relationships.
4. Learn good communication.
5. Evaluate strengths and weaknesses in communication.
6. Get the training you need.

FROM THIS DAY FORWARD

1. I will communicate better by listening more and concentrating on the other person's problems and ideas.

2. _____.

3. _____.

4. _____.

CHAPTER 3

THINK 110 PERCENT

Hard work is the best investment a man can make.

—C. M. Schwab

THE THIRD LAW FOR GETTING A GOOD JOB IS HAVING A STRONG WORK ETHIC!

Workers who show up on time, are productive, and enjoy going that extra mile inevitably get the promotions over workers who show no enthusiasm or dedication to the job. After decades of socialism, Russian workers find it difficult to go the extra mile because there has been little or no incentive to do so. Even though their economy is shifting to a free enterprise system, it will be tough for these workers to make the transition to a new work ethic. In the U.S., we have had more than two hundred years to encourage a strong work ethic, and that is precisely what employers have come to expect.

You can verify the truth of this important law by answering the following questions:

- If I am paying someone to paint my house, do I want the painter to do a quick job, a mediocre job, or a thoroughly professional job including cleanup?
- If I'm paying someone by the hour to repair my automobile, how often would I want him to take breaks or chat with coworkers?
- When I've employed someone to repair my plumbing, do I expect it to be halfway, mostly, or totally fixed?
- If someone agreed to cut down a tree for $200 then asked for $250 after the job was finished, how would I feel?

Your answers are the same as everyone else's. We expect to get our money's worth from people we pay to render a service. Companies and corporations deserve the same from their employees. After all, businesses are owned and operated by people just like the rest of us. I have participated in the recruitment for scores of companies that were expanding or relocating their businesses, and the work ethic of available employees is always a top concern. In fact, the ability to get a well-trained workforce with a strong work ethic is the number one incentive for new, expanding, or relocating businesses. American businessmen and businesswomen recognize that people make their company successful or unsuccessful, and that is why training and the work ethic are so important to them. The only way businesses can survive in the global marketplace is to outproduce or outservice their competitors. And the only way they can outperform their competitors is through the use of excellent workers, workers who are willing to give 110 percent all the time.

The Profit Factor

In a free market economy, your ability to compete in the marketplace determines whether you make a profit or lose your shirt. Employers understand this fundamental principle, and they are interested in workers who also understand it. Private employers look for employees who understand that *profit* is not a dirty word and that job security is directly tied to their productivity. As cruel as it sounds, no one owes anyone else a job or even the chance for a job. Further, no workers should feel entitled to promotions or salary increases unless their productivity and worth to the organization increase. You have to earn your job by preparing for it and keep your job by helping the employer make a profit. In short, your ability to outproduce your competition ultimately determines your success on the job or in a career.

In today's global economy, we can depend on one common truth: If a society wants to live well, it must produce well. I would take this truth one step farther and state, If you want to live well, you must produce well. You see, people and their ability to outproduce their competitors really drive the economy. Government does not drive the economy, and neither do corporations; people drive it. Subsequently, individual productivity is directly related to individual economic success, just as the collective productivity of a company is directly related to the company's economic success.

It is natural for us to want the highest salary we can get, to be appreciated for our work, and to be a part of something important. Most American employers are willing to provide these job satisfactions if we are willing to contribute our best toward making the business successful. Employers want workers to show up on time, give it their best every day, be honest and loyal, and go that extra mile for the company. That is what having a strong work ethic is all about; that is what employers expect and deserve. Believe me, when employers look at job applicants, they attempt to discover any information that reveals the applicant's work ethic.

As I review a job applicant's cover letter, application, or resume, I look for evidence of strong or weak work habits. For instance, has the applicant changed jobs often, and if so, why? Has the applicant been promoted repeatedly? And what do the references say between the lines? During interviews I concentrate on what really motivates the applicant: Work or play? Helping others or making personal achievements?

Does the person have a positive or negative attitude? Asking an open-ended question like, "What is one of your most gratifying career successes (or failures)?" is useful in gaining an insight into the applicant's work ethic. Before I employ people, I want to be convinced that they will improve the organization by being in it. I want to be convinced that they have integrity, are dependable, are team workers, are competent, are diligent, will be loyal to the organization, and will always give their very best at work.

What's the Motivation?

Worker motivation surveys consistently indicate that we are motivated by three primary factors:

1. Recognition
2. Being part of the team
3. Fair compensation

These job satisfaction factors are listed in priority order. Most employers and their human resource personnel recognize the relevance of these factors and are alert to how prospective employees approach them in conversation. For instance, if an applicant's major focus seems to be on compensation and benefits, he or she will not fare nearly as well as the applicant who wants to know more about the company and how he or she can become a part of it. Many of the more progressive American companies, including foreign-based companies operating in America, include their employees in the screening and interviewing process. Why? Because new employees will become coworkers, and coworkers can affect the productivity of the work unit or team. Often, a worker unit is compensated by its productivity. In this environment a strong work ethic is essential for every member of the team. One TRANE Corporation division, located in Pueblo, Colorado, allows each work team to screen, interview, and employ persons for all open positions. The company really understands the significance of getting good workers and making them part of the organization.

An anonymous, but wise, author once said, "There's no traffic jam on the extra mile." Therein lies a golden opportunity for you when you seek a job. Knowing about the law of 110 percent, you can design your application materials and your interview responses to emphasize your positive work habits. Of course, employers readily acknowledge the truth in Stanley J. Randall's quotation that "the closest to perfection a person ever comes is when they fill out a job application." The point is, you must be honest about your performance as well as your intentions.

A simple reference check with a former employer will often get at the truth. If you have had work ethic problems in the past, explain the situation and commit to becoming the most diligent, loyal, and productive worker the company has ever had; then follow through with that commitment. Each new job is an opportunity to move past a former work performance record and establish a better one. If you have had a good work record, talk about it and be proud of it—this will probably get you the job. If you are a first-time worker, resolve to give it 110 percent right from the beginning and tell the interviewer about your resolution. Ask the interviewer how you can best become a valued employee. He or she will be impressed.

Diligent Workers

Just how important is work ethic? Consider Joseph of biblical times. His brothers sold him into slavery, and penniless and friendless, he was taken to a foreign land. With hard work, integrity, and loyalty, he rose to national prominence and saved his family from starvation.

Or think of Andrew Carnegie. As an impoverished thirteen-year-old, he entered the U.S. with his family. Through being diligent, persevering, and going the extra mile at work, he became one of the country's wealthiest men. From the age of fifteen, he was continually promoted until he began his highly successful steel-making business.

Perhaps the modern-day epitome of someone with a strong work ethic is Lee Iacocca. His career pursuits were not always easy, but his determination and hard work eventually paid off handsomely. After thirty years of working for the Ford Motor Company, Iacocca was fired. Undaunted, he became the chief operating officer for the Chrysler Corporation and wrestled it from near receivership and annihilation into national prominence and respect. Lee Iacocca represents a very good example of a strong work ethic and the 110 percent law.

Conclusion

Just as you expect your automobile mechanic to fix your car promptly and reliably for a fair price, employers expect to pay their workers a fair wage to be productive in a timely fashion, with quality work. If we, as workers, expect to be recognized for our efforts, appreciated by our coworkers, and compensated fairly, it's up to us to be the best at our jobs. It's up to us to put out 110 percent each and every day for the employer.

As a job seeker, you must emphasize your commitment to the company and underscore your strong work habits. Employers will continue to hire applicants who are most convincing that they will produce more for the company than their wages and benefits cost. Being honest, being a team player, getting to work on time, staying until the job's done, and being loyal to the company are all critical traits to communicate to a potential employer.

Practical Advice

The first impression successful job seekers always make on people, especially potential employers, is positive. Projecting a positive attitude about life and about work is essential. Communicating your enthusiasm for the job and the company is also important, and convincing potential employers that you have a strong work ethic is icing on the cake. The secret to making a great impression is to be all that you say you are. Be enthusiastic and positive, communicate well, and be a worker who is willing to give 110 percent every day.

When preparing application materials, write them in a manner that emphasizes your work ethics. Illustrate evidence of your commitment to the companies you have worked for by pointing to promotions, salary increases, or letters of commendation. A reference to your outstanding performance evaluations can also communicate that you are a good worker. Encourage your reference letter writers to emphasize your work ethic and productivity. All of your references really want you to get the job of your choice, and they will be pleased to emphasize whatever you ask, as long as it's true, of course.

Finally, point out your work ethic strengths when given the opportunity during the interview. Inevitably, you will be asked to tell about yourself. This is your cue to talk about your career goals and career successes. After the interview, you want the interviewer to feel she knows you and can trust you. You want the interviewer to believe his company needs to hire you before someone else does. Some chitchat about your roots, your family, and your training is appropriate, but focus most of your comments on your enthusiasm for your work. Let the interviewer know that you are looking for a quality company where you can grow by helping the organization grow into the best of its field and that you want to be a team player with people who aspire to be the best!

POINTS TO PONDER

1. Project enthusiasm.
2. Project integrity.
3. Project dependability.
4. Project cooperation.
5. Project competence.
6. Project diligence.
7. Project loyalty.
8. Give 110 percent.

FROM THIS DAY FORWARD

1. I will work harder and smarter than my fellow workers.

2. _____.

3. _____.

4. _____.

CHAPTER 4

FORGET THE
LONE RANGER

~~~

*If you don't believe in cooperation, just
observe what happens to a wagon
when one wheel comes off.*

—Anonymous

THE FOURTH LAW FOR GETTING
A JOB IS BEING A TEAM
WORKER!

In much of our early childhood we are taught to be
competitive, and we are rewarded for outperforming
our peers. We quickly learn to compare our performance to the performance of others, and our self-
images are developed in this way. It is no wonder that
teamwork comes as a shock to many of us as we enter

the work environment that demands cooperation. With few exceptions, mostly in the arts, our jobs require good social skills and the ability to work as part of a team.

You can apply personal examples to verify the truth of the law of teamwork. Ask yourself the following questions:

- Have I ever seen an effective organization that did not have a common purpose and good teamwork by its members?
- Is it possible for me to build a Delta II rocket by myself?
- How many loners have I really enjoyed working around?
- Would I rather work with a brilliant, but independent, coworker or an average, but collaborative, coworker?

Most people are fired from their jobs because of poor performance, right? Wrong. Most people are fired because of an inability to get along with others. Being caught in a downsizing effort is happening to thousands of workers every year. In many of these situations, the company uses seniority or job category to determine who is dismissed. In other situations, the dismissal decisions are left up to the supervisors. In these cases, you can be sure the troublesome employees, that is, the ones who are least cooperative, will get the ax first.

The Need to Cooperate

Whether you left willingly, were fired, were forced into early retirement, or were downsized for lack of work, the interviewer for your next job will seek evidence that you were not separated because of an inability to get along with others. Your initial task, whether in the application materials or in the interview, is to remove all doubt from the potential employer's mind about whether you are cooperative. If you have been uncooperative in the past, explain what you learned from the experience, and then state your resolve to never repeat the mistake. Having a great attitude, communicating well, and displaying a good work ethic are critical, but if there is a lingering doubt about your ability to fit in and work well with others in the company, you will be eliminated from consideration. Take the initiative in explaining why you left your last job (without offering any criticism of that employer), and emphasize how you enjoy being part of successful work teams. After all, we usually spend more waking hours with our coworkers than we do with our families. Cooperation is essential not only for achieving a work goal but also for keeping a happy, healthy work environment.

"Just how cooperative should I be?" you may ask. Your employer or potential employer expects you to be as cooperative as it takes to get the work accomplished.

Several years ago my wife and I were interested in purchasing some land in central Texas. We were referred to a land Realtor named Big John and met him one rainy morning out in the hill country. Big John drove us out to the country off the back roads and onto a rarely used cow path. In shorter time than it takes to tell the tale, Big John's car slipped off the path into a four- or five-foot ditch. My wife and I learned about the consistency of the soil thereabouts after we trudged across a large recently plowed field to a home owned by Mr. Austin. After we spent a pleasant hour with Mr. and Mrs. Austin, the tow truck finally arrived, and Big John stepped out to make the arrangements. With a twinkle in his eye Mr. Austin leaned toward me and said, "You know Big John long?"

"No, sir," I replied.

"Well, me and Big John get along I reckon, but I do most of the gettin', you understand!"

We did not buy any land from Big John.

The point to the story? If you want that job and if you want to keep it, be sure you do most of the gettin'.

Balance Between Task and Team

People will happily volunteer good references if they are deserved. Although most people are cautious about giving negative references, potential employers are very attuned to what is *not* said. If you are not sure about your ability to get along with others or whether you are perceived as a team player, reflect on your last or current job. Do people like you? Do your peers invite you to lunch? Do you share credit for tasks well done but accept responsibility for problems? Some people, particularly high achievers, are naturally more task oriented than team oriented. They tend to be loners at the workplace. Achieving a proper balance between being task and team oriented is a worthy goal. (An exercise in Appendix A will help you determine if you have a healthy task versus team orientation.)

I once worked with an absolutely brilliant man who could accomplish almost anything, as long as no one got in his way. People marveled at his passion for life and for his work. His peers appreciated his talent and admired his innovative ideas. His superiors—and I was one of them—loved his work as an individual, but were continually worried about whom he would offend next. Unfortunately, the talented individual could not work well with any ideas except his own. In consequence, he often felt it necessary to confront others about their "lousy" ideas and "stupid" opinions. Poor fellow; the last I knew he was jumping from job to job and being completely misunderstood and underappreciated.

The law of teamwork is fundamental to your success at getting the job you want. Resolve now to talk less, listen more, criticize less, and praise more in every situation. You will feel better, and people will love you. Consider the best conversationalists you have known. Without exception they will be people who listen well and with patience. When you were a youth, getting the credit for some outstanding feat or performance was integral for the development of a healthy self-image. Some people are so insecure that they continue to strive for all the praise and all the glory, even when the achievement could not have been accomplished without the assistance of others. At the workplace, it does not really matter who gets the glory as long as the work team is recognized. It's the old "you reap what you sow" principle at work here. As you praise others, praise will be returned. When you get your next job interview, use this "listen more, praise more" attitude.

Working as a team player also means contributing more than your fair share and being willing to try other people's ideas even when they make little sense. The interviewer needs to envision you as a contributing, amenable employee. You can communicate this notion by describing some of your past career successes that involved a team effort. You may mention your individual leadership experiences but be certain to praise the team for the achievement. I assure you, such remarks will not go unnoticed by the interviewer.

Some Team Players

Roger Staubach rose to preeminence in the football arena as a Hall of Fame quarterback for the Dallas Cowboys. Years after his retirement media announcers and fans continue to talk about him. He was one of the greatest athletes the National Football League ever produced. Yet, the famous quarterback will be the first to tell you that the team and the coaches made him successful. Like all truly successful team sport heroes, he recognized that it took everyone working together for the team to have winning seasons.

The American people highly esteem General Colin Powell, commander of the allied forces in the Persian Gulf War. The national media gleefully speculated about a political career for the general. I recently attended an event where General Powell was a keynote speaker. He accepted credit for the outstanding success of that war on behalf of the men and women who fought it. He understands the value of teamwork and recognizes that working with people is essential to achieve any mission.

Conclusion

Employers and their human resource personnel know full well that a job applicant's ability to get along with others at the workplace is a critical skill. They know that a major part of their task is to employ people who will complement the workers already on the payroll. During the screening, interviewing, and reference calling, these decision makers will try to get a fix on your ability to work well with others. The more you can convince them that you are a team player, the better your chances of being employed will be. To be sure, employers are interested in leaders, especially leaders who can motivate others, but make no mistake about the law of teamwork. Ignore this law and you will spend a lifetime looking for the next job.

Practical Advice

Whether you are a good team player does not really matter if you are self-employed or financially independent. But if you are like the rest of us, you should be honing your social skills continuously. Learning to listen, praising others, and trying out the ideas of others are skills we can all learn and continue to improve. Try them at home with your family and with your friends. Before long, unless you are already expert at these skills, people will wonder what has come over you. Better yet, as you make a consistent effort to improve these skills, they will become second nature to you just when you need them most—during the job interview!

During a crucial part of the Second World War, General Dwight Eisenhower was told that his command desperately needed second lieutenants. There were no junior officers to be had, but General Eisenhower solved the problem quickly by ordering second lieutenant field commissions upon soldiers who were Eagle Scouts. The general was aware that the Scouts would know about leadership and teamwork, both basic characteristics for military officers. The general knew that the first part of the Boy Scout Law, for instance, required them to be "helpful, friendly, courteous, kind." Job seekers will do well to follow the same code. Being helpful, friendly, courteous, and kind just about wraps it all up if you want to get and keep a dream job.

Zig Ziglar, one of America's best motivational speakers and writers, reminds us that we can reach our successes if we help others reach theirs. It's the same at the workplace. We cannot expect to be successful alone. Come to think of it, even the Lone Ranger had Tonto to help!

POINTS TO PONDER

1. Do most of the gettin'.
2. Learn to listen.
3. Learn to praise.
4. Try others' ideas.
5. Illustrate success through teamwork.
6. Be helpful, friendly, courteous, and kind.

FROM THIS DAY FORWARD

1. I will be congenial and cooperative with my fellow workers.

2. _____.

3. _____.

4. _____.

CHAPTER 5

PS IS CRITICAL

—∞∞∞—

It is better to light a candle than to curse the darkness.
—Ancient Chinese Proverb

THE FIFTH LAW FOR GETTING A JOB IS BEING A PROBLEM SOLVER!

Employers are constantly on the lookout for people who can solve day-to-day problems at work. By adopting this law as a work habit, you will have no problems getting and keeping a job. Setting and achieving work-related goals are always desired, but a worker who has the ability to solve problems is most valued by employers.

You can easily verify the truth of the PS (problem solver) law by considering the following questions:

- Which person would I rather have to take care of my lawn: one who cuts and trims only, or one who cuts, trims, feeds, seeds, and does whatever is necessary?
- Which automobile mechanic would I prefer: one who replaces parts according to symptoms, or one who searches out the cause before replacing parts?
- Which employee do I think would be most valued: one who says, "That's not my job," or one who says, "Let's see how we can fix this"?

Obviously, an employer prefers to employ people who have the confidence, ability, and personal incentive to solve problems. Anyone can dodge responsibility at the workplace by ignoring problems or by suggesting that problems are not his responsibility. However, those who want to do well in a career and those who never need to worry about getting a job will take on the challenges as they occur.

An Opportunity to Learn

Only shortsighted people view the job as a means to survive. Truly successful people see each job as an opportunity to learn and to become the best at that vocation. People with the "it's not my job" attitude will likely never find satisfaction at work or anyplace else for that matter. Job interviewers are always alert for signs of such an attitude, and when they suspect people have it, they write them off permanently.

As a college student, I worked full time at a television station, as a technical engineer. I ran the cameras, audio board, film chain, videotape machines, and video board as assigned. I had to join a national labor organization to hold the job. One evening, while we were shooting a live commercial for an appliance store, a new television set began to slide off a shelf to the floor. A cameraman quickly steadied the television set whereupon a more seasoned employee chastised him. "That's not your job!" he bellowed. "Only the floor crew can touch things on the set. If you start doing things like that, they'll think they don't need a floor crew and we'll lose our jobs." You can buy into this attitude if you like, but it will be a violation of the PS law, and your chances for getting and holding a good job will be severely restricted.

As a seasoned college president, I can spot problem solvers at my very first meeting with them. They have a special notion that they are part of the organization, and they delight in putting its goals above their own. They talk about solutions and opportunities to improve the college and its students rather than about problems and potential problems. They are optimistic, cheerful, cooperative, and customer focused. They recognize the importance of the job, no matter where it is in the organizational chart, and they take pride in it.

Unfortunately, most people generally take their problems to their supervisor rather than attempt to solve them on their own. This behavior does not make them bad people; they are just doing what most American organizations have taught them to do for the past one hundred years. The old organizational hierarchy often emphasized process over results. These days most of us in positions of authority are trying to develop a new work environment. We try to empower people to take the initiative, to solve problems, and to make decisions on their own. The old hierarchical organizational model is no longer efficient or sensible. In short, we are looking for problem solvers.

Initiative, Imagination, and Ingenuity

Just how do you learn to practice the attributes of this law? First, you should clearly understand the organization's vision. What does the company really want to become or accomplish? Once you understand the vision or major company goal, you should learn the parameters of your job, including how much latitude and responsibility you have for completing your tasks. Second, you should learn to exercise the three *I*'s: initiative, imagination, and ingenuity.

Take the initiative when problems emerge. It is okay if it does not work out right the first time or even the second or third time. The point is that you are willing to take the risk, to be the leader in a difficult situation. Besides, opportunity seldom comes to us on a platter;

it's usually disguised as a major problem. Problem solvers also use their imagination. They enjoy thinking outside the norm. They solicit input from others and from as many sources as possible. They never lose the childhood excitement of discovery. There is no substitute for ingenuity. Being resourceful and clever about finding solutions to problems for the ingenious is a creative process. Each problem or difficulty can be approached as an opportunity to be innovative, an opportunity to assist the company in reaching its vision.

You do not have to be working to practice the PS law. Indeed, the best place to improve your skill at this law is at home. Opportunities to solve problems at home are bountiful, from making plumbing repairs to helping settle domestic disputes. In truth, you have been solving problems and fixing things for years. The secret to becoming a good problem solver at work is adopting the same attitude, confidence, and skills you use at home. As you begin to think of yourself as a problem solver, you will remember workplace achievements that involved surmounting difficulties. Cite them in your application materials, if appropriate, and emphasize them during your interviews. Share the credit with your coworkers, but let potential employers know how you contributed and when you led the team.

Leadership

Leadership is a major part of the PS law. Leaders have the confidence to try new things, motivate people to work as a team, and accept the responsibility of failure. Leaders understand that failure is only an event. Someone once said that if at first you do not succeed, you are running about average. No one succeeds at everything. Sure, Ulysses S. Grant was a great general and went on to become the eighteenth president of our country, but before the Civil War, he was unsuccessful in the military and in business. As you plan your approach for getting a perfect job, include a resolve to demonstrate your leadership skills at every opportunity. Let the people you network and interview with know that you are not afraid to take leadership roles in solving problems. Let them know you believe in sharing praise, but you can accept the blame alone if something goes wrong.

Famous Problem Solvers

Former President Franklin Delano Roosevelt exemplified the character of a problem solver. He served as president of the United States from 1933 until 1945. During that time, he led the nation through the worst depression and the most extensive foreign war in our country's history. His methods for stabilizing the country's economy and leading the war effort are still debated, but everyone concedes that he was a dynamic leader and an excellent problem solver. He faced formidable odds, including a physical disability, but he never ceased to use his resources to find solutions for the organization (country) he ran. He faced adversity with optimism and stress with unconcern.

Another famous problem solver received the Presidential Medal of Freedom in 1977, but he refused all cash awards for himself. Jonas Edward Salk created the polio vaccine at the University of Pittsburgh in 1953, and this terrible disease, which killed or disabled hundreds of thousands each year, has been virtually eradicated from the earth. Dr. Salk used all the resources and staff at hand to fix a problem for untold millions of people now and in the future.

Not all of us can become as famous as Roosevelt or Salk with the solutions we discover. But each of us, solving one problem at a time, is contributing to the betterment of the organizations for which we work, the economy, and ourselves. Most important, by assuming the character of a problem solver, we increase our chances for employment success.

Conclusion

Employers are looking for people who will take the responsibility to solve problems. They are eager to employ people who will take the initiative to improve on processes, services, or production to help the company increase profits and reach its vision. Wise job seekers acknowledge the importance of the PS (problem solver) law and seize opportunities to demonstrate initiative, imagination, and ingenuity. Successful job seekers exhibit leadership skills by demonstrating belief in themselves and in the value of teamwork. Above all, successful problem solvers continually ask themselves how they can help the company improve.

Practical Advice

Whenever the opportunity presents itself, during networking, with application materials, or in the interview, flaunt your experiences in problem solving and in applying leadership skills. Let the interviewer know that you believe in solving problems as they occur, and when problems need to be bumped up the ladder, you will present some recommended solutions. Corporate America is pushing decision making to lower levels to achieve better efficiency and productivity. The demand for employees who think for themselves and are not afraid to look for solutions is increasing.

Remember, talk with confidence about your ability to handle tough problems and stressful situations in a teamlike fashion. Share the credit for past successes at solving work problems, but make it clear that you often led the team. Finally, make sure any prospective employer knows that you relish solving problems and helping your organization meet its goals.

POINTS TO PONDER

1. See problems as opportunities.
2. Project initiative.
3. Project imagination.
4. Project ingenuity.
5. Be a leader.
6. Believe in yourself (and others).

FROM THIS DAY FORWARD

1. I will trust my instincts and attempt to solve problems at work as they occur.

2. _____.

3. _____.

4. _____.

CHAPTER 6

SERVICE LEADS TO SATISFACTION

———◦◦◦◦———

Those who bring sunshine to the lives of others cannot keep it from themselves.

—Sir James Matthew Barrie

THE SIXTH LAW FOR GETTING A JOB IS BEING CUSTOMER FOCUSED!

We all like to be treated with dignity and respect, especially if we see ourselves as customers. Employers are acutely aware of this consumer expectation, and they desire to have customer-focused employees. Violating this service law will guarantee unemployment.

There has been a revolution in management-labor relations in the United States over the past six to eight years in regard to this notion of better customer service. The total quality management and continuous quality improvement movements have centered on quality production and services to make American businesses more competitive. Corporate America has adopted a "new" service philosophy that really isn't new at all. Yes, it has a new name, but the principles of quality service haven't changed since the beginning of trade among humans.

Human nature has not changed much over the years, and consumers today wish to be treated well, just as consumers of the first century wished to be well treated. You can verify the truth of this law by answering the following questions:

- Do I like prompt and pleasant table service when I dine out?
- When the cable television or telephone is on the blink, which would I prefer talking to: a recorded voice or a real person?
- When I have some questions about my child's scholastic progress, would I prefer a defensive or receptive teacher on the other end of the line?

If we really want to know what type of employee most businesses are looking for, we merely have to visualize someone who impressed us with service. Learning to treat others as we like to be treated is the secret to this service law.

Two Types of Customers

But I want to work in manufacturing or engineering where I seldom come into contact with customers, you may be thinking. Guess what? Your work will eventually come into contact with the customer, and it will affect the image of your company. Furthermore, you will work with a host of internal customers each day. Most American workers have two major types of customers, external and internal.

External customers are the people or companies that purchase your products or services. Internal customers are people you work with in the production of products or services. Each customer is equally important. Without good service to external customers, your company will go out of business. Without good service to internal customers, production will diminish, quality will suffer, and your company will go out of business. All employees of a business, no matter what type of business, must be ever conscious of who their customers are and aspire to serve them well.

During my first few weeks of a new presidency at a large community college, I discovered a serious lack of external customer sensitivity. As I drove through the campus early one rainy morning in January, I noticed hundreds of students huddled under eaves and backed against buildings in lines stretching two blocks and more. I quickly phoned my assistant and asked if there had been a bomb scare. "Oh, no," she said with a laugh. "This is the beginning of a new quarter, and those are students registering for classes." After parking my automobile I went directly to the vice president for instruction and discussed the matter. "Isn't it great!" he replied to my inquiry about the long lines. "This means we've all got jobs next fall," he quipped.

I realized that he was sincerely proud of the long lines. They were a visible expression of how well the college recruitment process was working. I had a strong inclination to make the people responsible for abusing our customers (students) stand in the lines, also. Fortunately, my staff saw the light. To the credit of the vice president and many other fine people, that was the last quarter any student had to stand in long lines (or the rain) to register for classes.

The Boss as a Customer

Most workers understand that the boss is also a customer. They will go to great lengths to please her. In reality, all people they work with deserve the same considerate treatment since they are also internal customers. It takes the cooperative efforts of everyone in a business to make the business profitable and effective.

Several years ago, while serving as a vice president of a small community college, I needed a secretary desperately. I had finished writing a federal grant that had to be postmarked that day. I needed to have typed a cover letter and an executive summary of the grant proposal. It was after five o'clock, nearly everyone had gone home for the evening, and I was inept with word processors (a clear violation of an essential law—see chapter 11). After a frenzied look throughout several buildings, I found one secretary still at her desk. I scarcely knew her name, but I pleaded my case. She smiled, took the cover off her word processor, and asked how she could help. After calling her family, she dived into the work and was finished in less than half an hour. At that point, I was a customer to that secretary, and she recognized the importance of the activity to the college. I sent her a note and a couple of roses.

Two years later I was selected as president of the college, and the existing administrative assistant to the president moved to another state. Guess who I promoted to the open position?

The point of this service law is obvious. All employers are eager to hire people who value customer service and demonstrate the ability to be customer focused, both externally and internally. Customer satisfaction equates with successful careers and job security.

Cheerful Servers

Rotary International, one of the world's largest service organizations, hails a creed that states, "He profits most who serves best." The undeniable truth of this motto is verified daily in the lives of people all over the globe. Consider Mother Teresa. She is credited with being a living example of agape, or the most selfless love. Her service to humanity is legendary, and the peoples of the world respect and revere her. Why? Not because of wealth, position, athletic ability, or beauty, but because of her service and commitment to others.

One of the largest employers in the United States earned worldwide fame by being the best of its kind in customer service. McDonald's Incorporated captured the nation's hamburger market by focusing on customers. The company produced a good hamburger, then packaged and sold it in a more convenient manner than anyone had done before. McDonald's led the way for the fast-food industry in this country and is doing the same in countries throughout the world. How did it become a giant corporation that is still known for its leadership in the hospitality industry? By focusing on customers.

The history books and the American public will long remember former President Jimmy Carter with affection and admiration because of his sincere commitment to serve people and to promote peace. His leadership in Habitat for Humanity is inspiring. His leadership in promoting peace throughout the world is now legendary. The one personality trait that has made him internationally famous is his humility as he serves others.

We're All in the Service Business

All successful job seekers and job keepers understand the importance of service to others. Whether they are directly serving external customers or working with coworkers, these successful people know the value of service above self. To them, cheerful service becomes a way of life, an attitude of endless commitment to helping others, a distinguishable part of their identity. I can assure you that interviewers can sense this personality characteristic within the first minute or two of an interview.

"But I'm in the manufacturing business, not the service business," you may say. Baloney. We are all in the service business, no matter what we do or where we do it.

"But I am a loner. I don't like people much, and I cannot change the way I am," you may protest. Hogwash. We have the freedom and the ability to change an attitude about anything anytime we wish. As we change attitudes, our behaviors change, and we profit because of this conscious effort at self-improvement. And the best part about conscious attitudinal change is that it becomes unconscious behavior after a short while. In effect, we can reprogram our attitudes at will. Now that is real freedom!

Putting the service law into practice must become a way of life. It means that we continuously think about the needs of others and not just about the literal accomplishment of a job assignment. A colleague directed her maintenance people to put one hundred chairs underneath some trees on our college campus in preparation for an annual retirees' picnic. She was aware that standing for long periods would be prohibitive for many of the older people. Fortunately, she checked on this activity just before the event was to begin. Her subordinates had indeed placed the chairs under the trees, but they left them in the double-tiered storage racks. Their commitment to customer service was less than ideal. These workers had performed the literal task as assigned, never thinking about setting up the chairs for the college's esteemed guests. The men failed to understand the principle of the service law. "Service above self" is a good motto for people who want to find and keep good jobs.

Conclusion

Employers must have satisfied customers and satisfied employees. Employers are looking for people who genuinely care about serving others, both paying customers and fellow workers. Employers seek employees who understand that customer service is a virtue. Employers truly value employees who apply a customer service attitude eight hours a day, five days a week. Finally, astute job seekers will recognize that their service to others and their ability to get along with others are the best methods for job security in this insecure world of work.

Practical Advice

Remember, employers desire customer-focused employees. You can have the best credentials, the best skills, and the best intentions, but if you cannot serve your external and internal customers well, you'll be of little use to your employer. Being customer focused means more than just having a cheerful attitude. It means having a true commitment to serving others. In the world of work, serving others means helping others meet their needs and achieve their objectives sometimes in spite of your needs or standard operating procedure.

Putting the service law into action means thinking about the intent of the work assignment and doing your best to accomplish the goal as opposed to simply trying to get by with the least amount of effort. People recognize and appreciate service-oriented people. Your reputation for service to others follows you wherever you go. The next job reference may well be the one that helps or hurts you depending on someone's recollection of how you treated him or others around him.

POINTS TO PONDER

1. Service to others is a virtue.
2. Employers value customer-focused employees.
3. Customers include everyone, inside as well as outside the company.
4. Customer satisfaction equates with job security.

FROM THIS DAY FORWARD

1. I will be the most customer-focused employee in my work group.

2. _____.

3. _____.

4. _____.

CHAPTER 7

RESULTS, NOT PROCESS

*Our grand business is not to see what
  lies dimly at a distance, but to do
  what lies clearly at hand.*
  —Thomas Carlyle

THE SEVENTH LAW FOR GETTING A JOB IS BEING RESULTS ORIENTED!

In their milestone book *In Search of Excellence*, Tom Peters and Robert Waterman described America's most successful corporations as having a "bias for action." The corporate environment the coauthors described came from the people who worked at those companies. In other words, the most successful companies have workers with a bias for action, workers who are interested in results more than processes.

You can verify the truth of this successful job-seeking trait by asking yourself the following questions:

- When I or my child last needed medical care, was I more concerned with completing the health insurance verifications or with seeing the doctor?
- Have I ever been given the runaround by a company when I needed repairs on something still under warranty?
- Did I ever qualify for a badly needed loan only to be lectured about collateral, credit history, or my ability to repay it?

Most of us have experienced the frustration associated with one or all three of the above illustrations. As consumers, all of us are interested in immediate attention, no lectures, and no runaround. Is it any wonder that employers are always on the lookout for action-oriented, results-seeking employees?

If you have ever had to wait for an auto part or for a certain fabric to be available, you can understand why employers need workers who produce things on time. If customers cannot get what they want in a timely manner, they will take their business elsewhere. Employers understand this basic relationship between producer and consumer, and they want to employ workers who also understand this principle.

Getting Things Done

Employers desire customer-focused employees who can get things done. A cheerful, engaging attitude is nice, but it is not enough to become a sought-after employee. To get your dream job, you have to convince the employer or interviewer that you can get things done. You have to convince a potential employer that you will help the company make more money than your total cost of employment. In short, you are an enterprise that will accomplish tasks assigned in a results-focused manner. You understand how to work within the parameters of company policies and procedures, yet you know how to complete tasks in an exemplary fashion.

How busy you are and how busy you look have little to do with actual productivity or accomplishment. A person can be busy all day and all week, but never come to closure on anything of value to the organization. Work has a way of expanding to fill the time allotted for it. A number of productivity studies have proved this principle. The best employees consciously focus on accomplishing assigned tasks to the very best of their ability in a timely manner. These employees seem to have an intuition for being productive.

We've all witnessed people whose desks are overflowing with papers, reports, and books. Usually, their office chairs and tables are also loaded with paperwork. They think this office demeanor projects how important the job is and how hard they work. In reality, their office condition projects disorganization, confusion, and insecurity. Either they are thoroughly disorganized and inherently messy, or they are attempting to boast about how much work they do. In either case, such a display indicates that the workers are process-oriented persons as opposed to results-oriented persons. Results-oriented workers are eager to finish tasks and move the paperwork along. Results-oriented people have a strong need to close out projects and tasks and move to the next challenge. Their desks or work areas are generally kept clean and uncluttered to be prepared for the next task.

Character Flaws

Some workers are simply lazy. For some inexplicable reason these people would rather put off doing the work than jump into it. They are almost never productive. Even if they manage to get a job, their chances of keeping it are slim unless they have some type of labor protection. Such behavior is wasteful for the company and for the workers. Believe me, employers can spot lazy people faster than a speeding bullet.

I have known many lazy workers in my career, but the worst ones are almost always very intelligent. These folks work harder to keep from working than to do their assigned work in the first place. I have yet to find a good explanation for such behavior, but I have learned to identify these people with great accuracy. Most of them would make excellent employees if they could eliminate that one character flaw. The point? Companies or organizations exist by providing products or services. All employees must carry their share of the load if the employer hopes to stay in business. If you hope to land a cushy job where you do little work, you may as well throw in the towel now. You will be found out. Ignoring this law of action and results is one of the surest ways to stay unemployed.

There is one exception to this law, yet this exception is diminishing in the United States. Strong labor unions often protect workers from losing their jobs for most anything except violence or direct insubordination. As a young television station cameraman in the sixties, I well remember being criticized by my union "brothers" for working too hard. Their reasoning was that the company would expect everyone to be that productive if I kept working so diligently. They often advised me to carry a hammer around the studio and just look busy. That unfortunate experience illustrates how peer-imposed work behaviors can be destructive to initiative, ingenuity, and self-worth. If you intend to get a good job and keep it, you must present yourself at the interview and at the workplace as a results-oriented person who takes pride in helping the employer be successful.

Companies fail for many reasons, but the surest road to failure is for them to be noncompetitive because of poor production or poor service. All employees of a company can lose their jobs if a few workers fail to recognize that their ability to achieve results affects the profitability of the entire company. As you network for job tips or job referrals, project an image of a results-oriented, hardworking, enthusiastic person who looks for solutions, not excuses.

Everyone can find excuses for not getting the job done. Some people become experts at the art of excuses. They generally blame others, blame the equipment, blame the customers, blame the company, or blame some condition beyond their control for poor performance. In truth, we generally have no one to blame but ourselves for poor performance. Do not listen to others who help you find excuses or tell you some task cannot be done or is unreasonable. Above all, do not listen to yourself when you begin to think negatively. Successful job seekers and job keepers learn how to focus on completing tasks, no matter how difficult, with a positive mental attitude. When you network and apply for your dream job, avoid espousing excuses just as you avoid using profanity. Your reputation, especially when you are a worker in transition, must be impeccable. You never know who talks to whom about you and your job search.

Change May Be Indicated

If a work process gets in the way of progress, try to change the process. As I interview people for jobs, I am always alert to any response that reveals the interviewee's approach to such problems. I nearly always ask the interviewee to describe a past work problem and how he solved it. If the answer does not demonstrate initiative and a bias for results, I generally move to the next interview.

If I witness process-focused behavior with employees, I try to get them to shift that focus toward solutions and results. As president of a college, I often go to where our customers are being served to get an eyewitness account of our services. On one such occasion, at the beginning of a new semester, I saw two very long lines in the bookstore. Some lines are to be expected during this time since all students are buying new books and supplies for their classes. To my amazement, the students were standing for twenty or thirty minutes in the first line to present their book list and receive their books from a clerk. The students then stood in another line for twenty or thirty minutes to pay for the books! I asked for an explanation from the bookstore manager, but I was less than satisfied. After making a few suggestions and hoping that some creativity would emerge from the manager, her response was, "But that's how we always do it." You can imagine how much confidence I gained in that employee at that moment. When you get your job interview, be prepared to describe a problem with a process and how you solved it.

You can stay results oriented if you constantly remind yourself of your primary job. With rare exception, every job's primary purpose is to produce quality products or services for customers. When the process interferes with this primary purpose of your job, you have an obligation to change the process within your purview or request a change in the processes outside your purview.

In all problematic situations you should ask yourself two basic questions: (1) Is it good for the customers? and (2) Is it good for the company? If the answers are in the positive and your solution is legal, you will seldom be wrong, even if a particular procedure or process says otherwise.

Becoming process oriented is generally nonproductive and unbelievably bureaucratic. Take a look at the Internal Revenue Service if you want to experience process orientation at its worst. The IRS code alone has more than six million words, most of which are left to interpretation! Becoming process oriented is a trap that all aspiring and existing workers should avoid.

Busy People

When something needs to be done, who are the most sought-after people in your neighborhood or community? They are always the busiest people. Why? Because they have a reputation for getting things done. Hugh McColl, chief executive officer of NationsBank, is often asked to lead national commissions, state councils, and national and local fund drives. He is sought after because people know he gets things done. Yes, his powerful position helps him accomplish much, but that position was secured through years and years of getting things done in less-powerful positions. His operating style underlies his success. He built a banking giant by setting a vision, encouraging employees, and assigning clear expectations and objectives rather than telling people exactly how to accomplish the objectives. Most effective leaders, like Hugh McColl, learn to establish a vision, set broad operating parameters, and focus on results. They describe the outcomes they want without dictating the details for achieving those outcomes.

In the dark days of the United States Civil War, President Lincoln went through commander after commander of the Army of the Potomac before he commissioned Ulysses S. Grant to that high post. Grant had won the war in the West by taking Fort Henry and Fort Donelson, then winning at Shiloh and Vicksburg. Nevertheless, Mr. Lincoln received much criticism for the appointment. Grant was often criticized by jealous critics, but Lincoln swept away the criticism by explaining that he couldn't "afford to do without this general because he fights!" Grant had built his reputation for being results oriented, and that part of his character was most valued for the task.

Conclusion

Companies and people are valued for their ability to get things accomplished. Consumers appreciate and are willing to pay for quality products and extraordinary service. Employers seek workers who understand the importance of being results oriented, workers who have a natural desire to be productive and focus on the needs of the customer. Successful job seekers will put this law of action into practice not just during the interview, but in all things they do before and after getting a job. A distinct asset of an aspiring worker is a solid reputation for getting things done.

Practical Advice

Projecting a work ethic that includes a bias for action and an interest in achieving results will pay big dividends for job seekers and for workers who desire to be promoted. Successful workers avoid any behavior on and off the job that could damage their reputation as effective and valued employees. Laziness, negative thinking, and a bureaucratic mentality should be avoided at all costs. Remember, employers look for people who have a strong need for closure and who enjoy getting things done in a timely and professional manner. Employers are consciously seeking workers who think for themselves and focus on solutions rather than on problems. Throughout the job search process, whether you're networking with a friend or taking a formal interview, be sure to convince people that you focus on job results rather than processes.

POINTS TO PONDER

1. Have a bias for action.
2. Focus on results.
3. Have a strong need for closure.
4. Build a good work reputation.

FROM THIS DAY FORWARD

1. I will work for results and attempt to change processes that interfere with results.

2. _____.

3. _____.

4. _____.

CHAPTER 8

YOU HAVE TO HAVE A PLAN

———— ❧ ————

Order is light, peace, inner freedom,
self-determination: It is power.
—Henri Frederic Amiel

THE EIGHTH LAW FOR GETTING A JOB IS GETTING IT TOGETHER!

Setting a career goal or a specific job objective and developing and working a plan to achieve it are the essence of the getting it together law. If you have no career goal or specific job objective, you will likely be unhappy with the work you get. If you have a job objective but do not develop or work a plan to achieve it, you will fail. No one can reach a goal unless it has been clearly identified and it is accompanied with a plan for its accomplishment. In short, if you want a dream job, get your act together.

You can easily validate the truth of this law by considering the following questions:

- If I wanted to drive from Atlanta to Denver, would I consult a map?
- Would I rather have a well-organized or a disorganized teacher for my six-year-old?
- Do I prefer to fly with pilots who file flight plans?

Most people spend more time planning for a family reunion or a Fourth of July picnic than for their careers. Just a little planning can help you take advantage of the getting it together law. Planning and diligent effort are the keystones to career and financial success.

What Is Your Career Potential?

Choosing a perfect job or career can be frustrating and confusing. After all, your long-term success and satisfaction in the workplace depend upon this critical selection. Fortunately, many people eventually gravitate toward a career they enjoy. Many others, however, drift from job to job and never find one that is truly rewarding. Still others find themselves caught in a downsizing industry and must select a new career field to become employable.

You can take the guesswork out of the career selection process by understanding your job-related interests, values, and abilities. As you compare probable careers or jobs to your interests, values, and abilities, the identification of a career category and eventually a job objective become evident. Consider exceptional athletes or scholars. They first discover their unique interests and abilities, then they select the sport or academic area they most value. By capitalizing on their basic interests, abilities, and values, they practice to become exceptional. The same principle holds true for people who successfully match their special interests and skills to jobs that allow them to flourish.

Further, you should choose a career path that you really value. Frankly, it does not matter what others think you can do. What matters is what you think and truly wish to do with your life. I am in my eleventh year as a college president, I have a doctorate, and I have achieved national acclaim in some educational circles, yet two high school teachers told me that I was "not college material." You can be anything you wish to be if you want it badly enough and are willing to work hard.

Most people believe that IQ, grades in high school, and socioeconomic condition are the primary predictors of their future success. They are wrong. The most accurate predictors of future success include a moral character and a career vision with the desire and self-discipline to pursue that vision. Your personal motivation to reach a goal or to succeed at a vision will determine your career success. Your consistent zeal for and focus on the goal are paramount if you hope to achieve your personal career vision. For this reason, select a career goal that you truly value and fully expect you can accomplish. If you neither value nor expect to reach the goal, you will fail.

In the early seventies, I taught two young college broadcasting students whose academic conditions were dissimilar. John's performance in the classroom was uninspired. Gary's academic record was exemplary. John's grades dropped so that a colleague counseled with him. "It is obvious you are not very interested in your studies, John. Just what is it you would really like to do?" my fellow teacher asked. "I'd really like to make music," John replied. My colleague suggested that he should try it. A few years later John Cougar Mellencamp hit the charts as one of America's top rock and roll stars!

From my first meeting with Gary, he told me he was going to be the voice of the Indianapolis 500 and would be a television network announcer for auto racing. His grades were always outstanding, and he was graduated with a degree in broadcasting without a slip. A few years later, Gary Lee was recognized throughout the country as the ESPN anchor for auto racing.

What attributes propelled both young men into their nationally recognized careers? It was not their academic success or their economic status. The vision or career goal and persistence in achieving it were the attributes that made them so successful. They both set a goal that they highly valued and expected they could reach.

Of course, you must see yourself clearly and objectively. It is unrealistic to think you can become a professional baseball player just because you want to be famous and make a big salary. Even Michael Jordan, one of the greatest NBA players of all time, tried to make it in professional baseball but failed to excel in that sport. It is equally unrealistic to think you should become an astronaut unless you're willing to get the education and training required for that competitive career. If you exaggerate or minimize your interests or abilities, the result will likely be unpleasant. Be true to yourself when you select an immediate job objective or long-term career goal.

Stan Olsen, a founder of Digital Equipment and a highly successful land developer, gave me this prescription for success: "Do more of the things you do well and less of the things you're doing!" When determining your career goal, emphasize your strengths and match them with career possibilities. Your chances for success will improve considerably!

Hopefully you have an immediate job objective in mind. A little research should reveal your deficiencies regarding the job objective. I hope you understand that learning new job skills is to be expected, so you may as well acknowledge any skills limitations and take the proper steps to eliminate them. You can review any number of job skills directories at a library, but the *Guide for Occupational Exploration* is the most common. Some computer programs, such as Choices and SigiPlus, can help you with this activity. You could also use the resources of a college placement or career assessment office for this purpose, or you could pay a private job search agency to help you. Most large public libraries and virtually every community and technical college will have useful resources. In most cases, you will be able to make a reasonable self-assessment if the job you seek is similar to a previously held job. In any case, if you are unsure of the job's requirements or your qualifications, get advice from a professional. As you review the educational credentials required for each job, look at any special skills that also may be desired. The idea is to match your skills and credentials to those required by your job objective, then identify any academic, technical, or social deficiencies that you know you will have to correct. (Appendix B provides a career assessment process that will help you identify the career areas most suited to your interests, values, and abilities.)

Take note: Before you can accomplish anything, you must truly want whatever is to be accomplished. Motivation is linked directly to what you value plus your belief that you can attain it.

Current job growth trends in the U.S. help you narrow down the twenty thousand possible job categories to focus on your personal job objective and career goal. You can match your interests and abilities to dozens of jobs, but if a job doesn't truly excite you, you are probably wasting your time. Upon completion of this chapter you should be able to clearly identify the perfect job or career for you.

As the U.S. adjusts its goods and services to be competitive in the global marketplace, jobs will be changing by type and skills required for at least the next ten years. American businesses cannot compete with the cheaper labor forces in less developed countries to do the standard assembly jobs of the past. Mexican and Malaysian workers can assemble piece goods, including clothing, at less than half the cost demanded by American labor. However, niche market areas in manufacturing lend themselves to American assembly because we have the automated technology or the exclusive knowledge base to outproduce foreign labor. Further, the demand for American computer software and for our consumer services is increasing rapidly. In short, the United States will excel in highly technical jobs and in selected services jobs through the year 2005.

The following job trends were developed and reported by the U.S. Department of Labor in its *1996–97 Occupational Outlook Handbook*. Essentially, the Labor Department reports job growth and job decline in two broad categories: service-producing jobs and goods-producing jobs. The trends reported here represent the job growth or decline over the eleven-year period from 1994 through 2005.

Service-Producing Jobs	*New Jobs in Millions*
Business Services	3.7
Health Services	3.2
Education Services	2.3
All Other Services	2.2
Social Services	1.5
Engineering and Management Services	.85

Goods-Producing Jobs	*Percent Trends*
Construction	10.0
Agriculture, Forestry, Fishing	7.0
Manufacturing	-8.0
Mining	-27.0

You can find many additional sources for job trends at your local public or college library. Two publications for this purpose are *Vocational Biographies* and the *Encyclopedia of Careers and Vocational Guidance.*

Remember, trends are job predictions. World events, new technologies, and many other variables can change these trends quickly. The important thing to understand is that today's jobs and tomorrow's jobs require (1) mastery of the basic skills and (2) high-level technical skills. To be a successful worker in the U.S., you will have to be educated and be prepared to upgrade your skills throughout your lifetime.

As a side note, most new jobs will come from businesses with fewer than five hundred employees in the services sector. The demographics of tomorrow's worker are also changing. More women, members of minorities, and workers with disabilities are expected to enter the workforce, and the average age of the American worker is getting higher. The effects of these changes will likely produce the need for more efficient and effective training systems at the workplace. As young people enter the workforce, they will need quick start-up technical skills training, and older workers will need to upgrade their skills as automation expands and job tasks change. As a transitional worker, you can become highly salable by increasing your educational and technical skills while searching for your immediate job objective or long-term career goal. Surveys vary, but many employment experts agree that it takes an average of three to five months to land a job of choice. (Appendix E provides additional assistance in the selection of your immediate job objective or long-term career goal.)

Networking Effectively

Once you have a clear career goal and a plan for achieving it, you will increase your chances for success by learning to network with anyone and everyone who can help in your job search. Networking is a job-seeking skill that you can learn to do well. The secret is to become good at making friends. The purpose of networking is to help you get job leads, job referrals, and job interviews. Networking can also lead to formal and informal references, and it can provide a more thorough perspective to your job search. In effect, each person you talk to about your job interests has the potential to become a job consultant to you at no cost. Networking can be fun, exhilarating, and effective if you are prepared.

As you increase your opportunities to visit with old friends and meet new ones, you should be prepared with some straightforward answers. For example, your best friends will ask you why you are looking for new employment or what happened to your prior job. Others will want to know the situation but will be too polite to ask. Think through this inevitable question, formulate a truthful, but positive answer, and volunteer it to people who may be able to help you. If they think you are hedging or keeping the full truth from them, the trust level of the relationship will suffer, and you will receive only superficial support. Do not be afraid to tell people you are out of work or about to be out of work. Being a transitional worker in the U.S. is more of the norm than the exception. There is no disgrace in being out of a job. The disgrace is in not looking for one! Just look them in the eye, be sincere, and be their friend. Avoid apology as you would boasting. Do not criticize your former employer, but let people know you are looking forward to the prospects of a new and rewarding job where you can really help your employer.

The most positive networker I have encountered in recent years visited his friends and his friends' friends, met community and business leaders, and wrote thank-you notes galore. But what impressed me most was his attitude. At the end of each conversation about his job search efforts, he would state, "Remember, I'm going to make the company that hires me a whole lot of money!" You see, you are not an out-of-work person desperately seeking a job; you are a valuable enterprise with the skills someone will be grateful to get.

To be an effective networker, you should take every opportunity to be with people and to win friends who can help you. Becoming a good communicator is relatively easy if you follow this formula for successful communication: listen, listen, and listen some more. Most of us have two ears and only one mouth. God had good reasons for this configuration. Invariably, study after study on communication indicates that the best communicators are those who have the patience and wisdom to listen. That means listening before responding, avoiding interrupting the speaker, and listening some more. This one communication skill can do wonders for your job search activity. You should also ask how you might be able to help those with whom you are networking. Building relationships is the key to this job search activity.

Occasionally, you will meet with people who do not speak freely. You need to find out about their interests as quickly as possible and focus on these things. If you are meeting someone on referral or for an interview, do some preliminary homework. Get a biographical description from someone who knows him. In this way you can get a feeling for his interests, and you can discuss your commonalities. The closer someone can connect with you, the more likely he will support you.

While in conversation, do not miss the chance to ask people for advice about your job search. Asking for advice is a sign of self-confidence, a sign of respect for the other person, and it is flattering. Once they give you advice, you must make every effort to use it and tell them how it helped. This situation will reinforce your relationship, and they will develop a greater commitment to your job search. It should go without saying that you should send a handwritten thank-you note to everyone who helps you even a little bit.

Finally, you should make a conscious effort to become as literate as possible with the issues surrounding your targeted job objective. You will become infinitely more believable as you become conversant about your sought-after profession. Read everything you can find about your career field, and talk, listen, and listen some more to people in that profession.

An Action Plan

Since getting a good job is a job in itself, you are prudent to approach the job search process in a professional manner by developing a plan and following it. This plan should be action oriented. That is, your job search plan should require you to take a series of actions, from writing your resume to preparing for final interviews. The following components make up an effective action plan:

1. Set up a job search center.
2. Develop contact lists.
3. Develop a filing system.
4. Develop a social calendar.

5. Develop a follow-through system.
6. Review job resources.

A job search center may be an office in your home, or it may be nothing more than a portable file box and the kitchen table. In any event, you will need to establish a job search center that is easily accessible, organized, and quiet. You will spend considerable time at your job search center writing letters and a resume, filling out applications, and writing thank-you notes. This center should have a filing cabinet or filing box, the tools for writing, a telephone, and a calendar as a minimum. A computer and printer would be nice, but you can purchase these services if you need to.

You should develop your contact lists as soon as possible. Companies do not hire people; people hire people. Your networking success will be tied to this list. Your list should include several categories of acquaintances who can help you with your job search. Your contact list categories should include old friends, new friends, relatives, referrals, and people you need to meet. (Appendix C provides a sample contact list format.)

You need to develop the lists, add to them as you meet more people or remember people you forgot, and keep notes regarding your contacts with each person. Your purposes in contacting these people include (1) telling them you are in a job or career transition, (2) asking them if they know of any job openings in your targeted job area, (3) asking them if they know of someone else who might be able to help you, (4) asking them for their advice regarding your job search, and (5) asking them to keep you in mind if they hear of anything relative to your job search. Make every effort to visit with your contacts in person, and follow up each contact with a handwritten thank-you note.

As you begin making direct contacts with potential employers, you will need easy access to the information relative to those contacts. Before you know it, you will be talking with a dozen or more potential employers, and the details of each contact will have a way of intermingling. By developing an information file for each prospective employer, you will be organized and prepared to recollect circumstances surrounding your involvement with each. (Appendix D provides a sample employer contact format.) Another file folder should hold your resume, sample letters of introduction, lists of references, academic transcripts, and other pertinent information for easy accessibility. Set up a final folder for storing all of your job search expenses. Most of these expenses are still tax deductible.

A social calendar keeps your networking organized and provides you the opportunity to do things with your friends that you were always going to get around to. Buy a pocket calendar and carry it with you at all times. Begin your networking plan by reviewing your contact lists and scheduling appointments with people you think can help you the most. Next, review all social events coming up in your community and schedule those that allow you to be with friends and prospective contacts or employers. You might even host a party or reception at your home. Remember, however, the purpose is to make friends at these events and not to become a pest with your zeal to get a job. A well-timed golf game, shopping trip, or other social activity with influential friends and acquaintances can do wonders for your job search efforts. Finally, consider becoming more visible. Volunteer for civic club activities, or get involved with the chamber of commerce, United Way, Boy Scouts or Girl Scouts, a church, or any other respected community activity. Involvement in such volunteer activities will diversify your contacts and will provide a welcome relief from the job search process. The more you help others, the more people will think of you when they hear of a job or have one coming open. Always dress appropriately, especially at social events and volunteer activities. You never know when you will come face-to-face with your next employer.

Developing a follow-through system is easy. In most circumstances, you will follow through with a note the same day someone agrees to help you. However, leave nothing to chance. A failure to extend a courtesy could retard your success. You should review your contact lists and information files daily. Each morning before making telephone calls or before getting ready for your appointments, you should catch up with the paperwork. Also, you should review what you promised yourself or others that you would do. Writing notes to yourself, perhaps in your pocket calendar, will help you establish a reputation for reliability and timely performance. Of course, you should always remember to thank secretaries or anyone else who helps you in any way. Cards are always appreciated.

Finally, you will need to review all available job resources regularly. You can get a list of the major employers in your community from the public library, from the property tax rolls, or from the business section of the telephone book. The local chamber of commerce can also be helpful. Almost all cities of any size now have an employment weekly that lists all jobs available in the region. Most libraries have databases for accessing information about all American corporations, and many are linked to national computer networks that can be good resources for identifying potential employers and available jobs. The Internet/World Wide Web is growing with information daily. Various networks accessible through Internet provide up-to-date job listings. You can generally access these listings through menu pages referring to *jobs, labor,* or *employment.*

Several job-related services will help you locate job listings, post resumes on employment networks, develop your own home page, and connect to commercial and noncommercial on-line information. Your local library or college will provide access to the Internet. Global Encyclopedia, just one of many networks accessible over the Internet, provides an on-line career center, and America's Job Bank is accessible through most states' job service database. Do not let this new cyberspace network deter you from getting the best job-hunting resources available. A local librarian will be able to assist you in this endeavor.

Each sizable community in this country also has a number of government agencies that can help with your job search. Social services, employment and training services, the Job Training and Partnership Act (JTPA) service delivery areas, and others can help. If you meet certain minimum qualifications, you can qualify for free training and job placement assistance. Within a year or so, one-stop career centers will be developed across the country that will consolidate the career assistance services of most government agencies. Of course, the local community, technical, or junior college can provide career assessment testing, training, and classes in the job search process. These colleges generally have job placement services for their students.

Finally, you could always contact a private employment agency or a career management specialist firm, often referred to as outplacement firms. The professionals in these organizations will know the job market in your area and can offer good advice. The employer often pays employment agency fees. Outplacement services generally require a fee either from your previous employer or from you. One last note of information, most professional employment agencies agree that the best jobs are often never advertised. Instead of going through the expensive and time-consuming process of advertising and screening applicants, many companies opt to contract with search firms to locate potential employees. This hidden job market is important to all serious job seekers. You will do well to network with private as well as public employment agencies.

Conclusion

Employers are looking for self-motivated employees who know what they want and are well organized. Successful job seekers reflect these same characteristics in the job search process. Envisioning a long-term career and targeting an immediate job objective go a long way toward achieving the getting it together law. Learning to network effectively and developing a job search action plan are also important for transitional workers. Being well organized projects confidence, reliability, and an impressive reputation to potential employers. You can display all the behaviors represented by the other eleven laws for getting a job and still be unsuccessful if you are disorganized. Ignoring this law will be disastrous.

Practical Advice

Getting organized—and staying that way—is the surest method for running an efficient and successful job search. Developing a job search center and using contact lists, a filing system, a social calendar, and a follow-through process make good sense. When you do get to the important job interview, you will have a definite advantage because you will have it all together, and that will be evident to the interviewer.

POINTS TO PONDER

1. Set a career goal.
2. Set a job objective.
3. Learn to network.
4. Develop an action plan.
5. Follow the action plan.

FROM THIS DAY FORWARD

1. I will plan my career strategy based on my ultimate career goal.

2. _____.

3. _____.

4. _____.

CHAPTER 9

PUT YOUR BEST FOOT FORWARD

~~~

Early impressions are hard to eradicate from the mind.

—Jerome

THE NINTH LAW FOR GETTING A JOB IS PUTTING YOUR BEST FOOT FORWARD!

Once you have determined your dream job and have developed a plan for getting it, you must focus your attention on the job of selling yourself. You must learn to put yourself in the place of all potential employers. They will be looking for evidence of the twelve essential laws for getting a job as described in this book. They will be looking for someone in whom they can have confidence, someone in whom their expectations can be met.

You can verify the truth of this job-seeking law by asking yourself the following questions:

- When I last bought an automobile, was the credibility of the salesperson important to me?
- When I last chose a bank, a physician, or a veterinarian, did the reputation affect my choice?
- When I hire someone to work inside my home, does the person's appearance matter to me?

Certainly, a person's credibility, reputation, and appearance are important to us when we consider purchasing goods or services from them. The same principle is true of employers and people in general. Self-esteem exhibits itself in many ways, and a healthy sense of confidence is important. But the impression you make on others is critical when you seek new employment.

As you network for a new job, consider everyone you come into contact with as potentially helpful in your job search. Always put your best foot forward. This is a small world, and your reputation depends on what other people think of you. Each person you meet presents an opportunity for you to build a stronger and stronger reputation. This reputation, especially when verified by an acquaintance of the employer, is a powerful asset for you as a job seeker.

As you begin to get interviews, you will want to put your best foot forward from the very beginning.

Interviewers usually have a number of technically qualified applicants, but they are looking for the person they think will best fit with the organization. Their impression of you will determine whether or not you get a job offer. Your job application, resume, and cover letter speak loudly about you. I selected one secretarial applicant over another principally because she was professional enough to type her application while the other applicant wrote it in longhand.

The First Sixty Seconds

The first sixty seconds of an encounter with a stranger are most lasting! There is much truth in the adage that we never get a second chance to make a first impression. Human beings are social beings. We exist in a world where our social experiences, that is our relationships with others, form the essence of our lives. All of us, employers included, have learned to develop instant opinions of other people based upon the way we perceive them through their personal demeanor.

It is your objective to sell yourself to the employer. In a real sense, you must view yourself as an individual enterprise. Almost everyone has a set of basic skills and talents that can be translated into meaningful employment if the employer has confidence in the applicant's ability to be productive in that particular work setting. The critical first sixty seconds can be your most important asset in getting a job if you know how to put your best foot forward.

Be Mentally Prepared

First things first. Many coaches are fond of saying to their athletes, "Get your head on straight." The same advice holds true in the job search process. Before every job query, job application, and job interview, you must project confidence, enthusiasm, and trustworthiness. Your comfort level in the interview will increase in direct proportion to your preparation for the event. To this end you should spend some serious time developing your career goal and an immediate job objective. Your personal plan of action should be tied to this job objective.

Your career goal is a vision of where you would like to be and what you would like to be doing with your life five, ten, and even twenty years from now. Your job objective is your next employment step toward that long-term goal. Your ability to clearly explain your career goal and job objective to a potential employer will affect your chances for getting the job. You need to know where you want to go in your career and how your career interests can help the employer meet his or her needs. For example, your career goal is self-centered, but your job objective as you relate it on paper and during interviews should be employer or company centered. Employers want to know what you can do for them, not what they can do for you.

Once an applicant spent five minutes in an interview telling me why the job she had applied for would be so important for her career aspirations. She never understood that I was more interested in what she could do for our organization than what we could do to further her career. Some people believe they are entitled to a job. But believe me, an entitlement attitude will guarantee job search failure.

Essentially, your job objective should state the type of position you are seeking and the contributions you hope to make to your employer. Unfortunately, a typical job objective looks like the following: *I am seeking a responsible sales position that provides opportunities for advancement,* or *I am seeking a challenging supervisory position in operations engineering.*

Both examples are applicant centered. They do not tell the employer what you can do for him or her.

A better job objective would be: *I am seeking a responsible sales position where my experience, energy, and diligence will produce higher profits for my employer,* or *I am seeking a supervisory position in operations manufacturing where my engineering and management experience can be used to increase corporate productivity.*

One caution: don't be so specific in the job title that you limit your employment possibilities. For instance, you might seek to become an office systems professional rather than an administrative assistant, secretary, or receptionist. It's probably safer to seek a leadership position in financial management than to seek a mortgage banker position. You can broaden your objective without losing sight of the goal and open yourself to positions you may not have originally thought about. (Appendix E provides an exercise designed to assist you in the development of your career goal and job objective.)

Be Spiritually Prepared

Being prepared mentally is essential, but it is often not enough. Successful job applicants are usually at peace with themselves, and they have enough faith in God and in themselves to sustain themselves during the job search process. Further, they accept rejections professionally with the understanding that rejections should not be taken personally. Finally, they have the heartfelt assurance that another job opportunity will soon evolve and that in the long run, all things happen for their good.

You can boost your spiritual preparation by associating with other persons of your faith and by reading Scripture. Two of the best methods for increasing spirituality are encouraging others and personal prayer. The self-confidence that usually results from a solid spiritual foundation is easily recognized by most employers through job applicants' attitudes, speech, and enthusiasm. Job applicants who are spiritually as well as mentally prepared have confidence and naturally put their best foot forward!

Be Physically Prepared

Seeking a job will require all the physical stamina you can muster. There will be stress and sometimes strenuous activity involved with the job search process, and you will want to be in the best physical shape possible. Besides, there may never be a better time to exercise and eat a proper diet.

Your appearance can be your best asset or your worst liability when you present yourself to people with whom you network and to the all-important interviewers. Your first impression will make a dramatic impact on them. The time to assess your overall visual and vocal impression is now—not a day or two before the interview.

It is sad but true; people treat you as they perceive you. Your first visual and verbal association with others will set off a whole series of judgments about your character and abilities. Even your handshake will project volumes about you. "But that's not fair," you may retort. Perhaps it is not fair, but people the world over process information and draw conclusions from that information the same way you pick car salespeople, physicians, or repairpersons.

Your dress, hygiene, breath, posture, grooming, body language, facial expressions, and speech contribute to your ability to make good impressions. You should display an attitude of alertness, vitality, and confidence under all situations associated with the job search. That includes informal times when people observe you without your knowledge.

Job seekers are well advised to develop their appearance according to that expected of people in the profession they desire. The most successful job seekers pay close attention to their initial appearance. Their clothing, hair presentation, and accessories are appropriate for an interview. Basically, they present a conservative appearance that does not detract from the information exchange process. Successful people also employ good posture, make frequent eye contact, and smile easily. Of course, they also converse easily and succinctly. If anything, all job seekers should be their best at dressing, posture, grooming, and articulating at all times.

Your speech should be natural with appropriate volume and clear diction. Having to exert a special effort to hear or understand you will make a negative impression on the interviewer. Certainly, eye contact and moderate smiling are essential elements for making good impressions. Don't play any power games by demonstrating your assertiveness or your ability to dominate. Be yourself, be courteous, be professional, and be in the best physical shape possible. Remember, you will be making impressions with everyone you meet, and you never know who or what group of people can help you reach your job goal.

Be Socially Prepared

Your whole attitude during (and after) the job search process should be to make as many friends as possible. People help people, and they usually help ones they know and like. The more friends you have, the better your chances for getting the job you want. A majority of job seekers are successful because of who they know, not what they know. Your ability to successfully network for job leads, referrals, and references will directly affect your chances for quick job acquisition. A big part of the job-hunting adventure involves socializing. This period in your life as a transitional worker presents a wonderful opportunity to socialize and make friends like never before. Smiles, good listening skills, and thank-you notes become tools in the socializing process.

Be Prepared for Tough Questions

Putting your best foot forward also means being prepared to answer the tough questions. Interviews generally create high anxiety for interviewees, but that anxiety can be reduced if you anticipate the tough questions and prepare for them. Most of these questions are designed to help the interviewer discover your values, work ethic, attitude, and ability to work with others, as well as your communication, analytical, and work-related skills competence. You should approach each question honestly and straightforwardly, always emphasizing one or more of the twelve essential laws for getting a job. Some standard questions include the following:

- Where have you worked in the past (i.e., describe work history)?
- Why do you want this job?
- Why did you leave your last job?
- Where do you want to be in five or ten years?
- What can you tell me about a career accomplishment?
- What can you tell me about a career disappointment?
- How do you usually handle angry people?
- Why are you the best person for this job?
- If I called your current or last supervisor, what would he or she tell me about you?

I interviewed a candidate for a high-level position who spent a full fifteen minutes describing his career in detail. I finally had to interrupt him to ask my second question, which concerned his career goal. His answer to that question was equally lengthy. He ended by stating that he would really like my job as president of the college and that he imagined I'd be retiring in a few years. Since I am still in my forties, he scored a zero for diplomacy. In any event, the applicant would clearly talk his coworkers to death. He did not get the job.

Conversely, another applicant for the same high-level position gave the shortest answers in history during the interview. She was very self-assured and was obviously well prepared for my questions. In fact, she was too prepared because her answers were like rehearsed sound bites for a camera interview. I tried to get her to relax and show me who she really was, but to no avail. There was no warmth in the personality, and her answers were so curt, I felt she was hiding something. She did not get the job either.

Conclusion

Putting your best foot forward is a sure way to achieving job success. Employers hire people they feel good about, people they like. Employers listen closely to friends, to references, and to applicants when making hiring decisions. Your ability to make a great impression before, during, and after the interview will determine whether you get the job. The first sixty seconds of the job interview are critical. Everything about you, especially your attitude, communication skills, and personal demeanor, plays a part in how the interviewer perceives you. Be mentally, spiritually, physically, and socially prepared for the interview. Anticipating job interview questions and having honest, believable answers will carry you to success.

Practical Advice

Projecting a positive, friendly attitude with a professional demeanor is a foolproof formula for job-seeking and job-keeping success. People hire and promote people who are productive and likable. Successful job seekers know how to be on their best behavior at all times, including during the interview. Successful job seekers are prepared to be successful in the job market, and they think of themselves as enterprises. Successful job seekers do not feel entitled to a job, but they are willing to earn a job by being their best before, during, and after their interviews.

```
┌──── POINTS TO PONDER ────┐
```

1. Learn to sell yourself.
2. Know what you want.
3. Be mentally, spiritually, physically, and socially prepared.
4. Recognize that the first sixty seconds are most important.
5. Be prepared for the tough questions.

FROM THIS DAY FORWARD

1. I will be my best in all social and work situations.

2. _____.

3. _____.

4. _____.

CHAPTER 10

LEARNERS: A PRICELESS COMMODITY

~~~

The education of a man is never completed until he dies.

—Robert E. Lee

THE TENTH LAW FOR GETTING A GOOD JOB IS BEING AN ACTIVE LEARNER!

Workers who cannot or will not continue learning risk becoming permanently unemployed. Transitional workers who are not active in learning new skills and new work behaviors will likely remain unemployed for a long time.

You can verify this law by asking yourself the following questions:

- If I owned a secretarial service and one employee refused or could not learn to operate the new, more efficient word processing software, would I (a) allow her to keep using the old software or (b) replace her with an employee who could operate the new software?
- I am interviewing equally qualified applicants, but one shows evidence of active learning throughout the career. Which applicant would have the edge?
- Which type of worker is most valued by the employer: a passive, methodical person or an active person who is eager to learn new work skills and techniques?

The correct answers are obvious, but they illustrate the point. The American workplace is changing rapidly, and the academic, technical, and behavioral skills required for workers in all fields demand continuous learning. Your willingness to gain new skills to be more productive at work represents the active learner law. Sometimes the learning curve, or demand for new skills acquisition, is steep (fast), and sometimes it is rather flat (slow). In either case, we are in a new environment that requires increased learning and new skills throughout our lifetimes as workers.

As a young boy in the 1950s, I was curious why our neighbor, a grizzled and reclusive older man we called Fuzzy, seemed to be so poor, yet never worked to earn any money. Our family of ten always had plenty to eat, but everyone worked. "Fuzzy has a rough way of it, son," my father explained. "You see, he used to be a well digger, but modern technology came along, and he didn't keep up with it, so he was pushed out of a job." That incident made a lasting impression on me. If anything, the changing technologies at the workplace today are occurring at lightning speed compared to the changes in the early fifties. We no longer live in a predictable world where we can expect to earn a living by the sweat of our brow. We no longer live in a world where we can expect to work for the same company in the same basic job until retirement. Just as poor Fuzzy was pushed out of a job for not learning new skills, today's workers are suffering the same fate with greater frequency. The tragedy is that it is not necessary to lose employment because of a skills deficiency.

The opportunity to learn new academic, technical, or behavioral skills has never been better. Most employers recognize the importance of keeping a well-trained workforce and encourage or even provide training for their workers. Community and technical colleges offer almost unlimited training opportunities, private training firms are bountiful, and many universities are expanding their outreach efforts. In short, if you need to acquire new skills, there is little excuse for not doing so.

American businesses spend $30 to $40 billion annually to train their employees. Business leaders expect to employ highly trained workers, but they realize that they will need upgraded training as technology and the competition change. Here are three emerging trends in this regard:

1. Management is providing more training for on-line workers.
2. Workers are managing themselves with less supervision.
3. Public higher education institutions are increasingly providing work-site education and training.

Further, by the year 2000 more than 75 percent of all jobs will require some education beyond high school, 23 million people will be employed in technical vocations, and nearly 50 million workers will need upgraded skills training to perform their current jobs. Learning has become a lifelong process, and we must continually upgrade our skills.

Shifting Workforce Skills

In the late 1970s and the early 1980s, national policy makers identified a skills shortage among American workers, especially young workers entering the workforce. Study after study indicated that the United States was last or near the last in academic preparation among the industrialized nations of the world. In 1983, *A Nation at Risk*, published by the United States Department of Education, made ominous predictions about the country's condition if our K through 12 educational system did not dramatically improve. We were losing our role as the most productive country in the world, and we had just slipped from the lowest to the highest debtor nation in the world. In the late 1980s, additional federal papers were published, including *America's Choice: High Skills or Low Wages* and *Workforce 2000*, which outlined the critical need for America's workers to become better skilled. Meanwhile, a Massachusetts Institute of Technology study on the loss of manufacturing jobs reported that if we wanted to live well as a nation, we had to outproduce our foreign competitors. We had emerged into a globally competitive society, and the requirements of our businesses and their workers have never been the same.

The mandate for all workers to become academically and technically skilled is clear. The requirement for workers to continuously increase their skills is equally clear. The responsibility for the acquisition of these skills is yours. I had an employee who refused to learn how to operate our new electronic mail system because she claimed she was too old to learn about such things. I also had an employee who still dictated in person to his secretary, refusing to use advanced technology for dictation or the composition of correspondence. Both people were great individuals with strong work ethics, but their productivity suffered because they refused to learn new workplace skills. I can assure you that employers everywhere in the U.S. are most interested in self-motivated workers who recognize that learning new skills is a necessary part of the job.

Today, our public K through 12 schools are doing better than they were in the late 1970s. Our students are scoring about average on academic tests compared to other industrialized nations. American workers are more technically proficient due mainly to the accessibility of training through community and technical colleges. Yet the skills shortage among American workers continues. There is a skills breach between worker preparation and employer expectations. Transitional workers who can fill this gap and meet the needs of the employer will have outstanding success in the marketplace.

If you wish to be among the most sought-after job applicants for any position, learn the behavioral and technical skills sought by employers, and make sure your prospective employer knows you have learned them. Of course, employers expect certain minimum academic and technical proficiencies, but their primary interest is in finding workers who exhibit behaviors that contribute to the success of the business or organization. As American businesses have learned to reduce supervision and increase worker autonomy, workers most valued have become those who have positive attitudes, can communicate well, can solve problems, and have a good work ethic. As modern employers attempt to push decision making to the lowest levels, they seek employees who take initiative and know how to make decisions. In effect, the skills most valued by employers are behavioral. That is precisely why ten of the twelve essential laws for getting a job are behavioral in nature!

You cannot ignore the final two laws, however. Having the specific academic and technical skills and the experience to do a job well is critical in most situations. As you develop your job objective and long-term career goal, you must identify what specific knowledge and skills you will need to get that job and to be successful in that career. You will need to develop an action plan to achieve the education required and become committed to it. People in your local college or skills training center will be more than happy to help you with this entire process.

By applying the active learner law, you will have a significant advantage over your competitors in getting the job you want. Certainly, employers look for evidence that you have a healthy appetite for learning new academic and technical skills. More important, they look for evidence that you have an enthusiasm to work effectively within the organization, can assume responsibility, and have the ability to motivate others to high performance.

Demonstrating Your Skills

The opportunity to demonstrate that you have the proper academic and technical skills required for a job is usually provided through questions in the job application. Degrees and certifications plus prior work experience are standard data requested in the application process. What is not often requested, but most desired, is evidence that you have the proper behavioral skills to make you a valued employee. The major purpose of the job interview is to discover what type of behaviors can be expected of you. You will improve your chances of getting an interview if you can demonstrate your behavioral skills in the application process.

First, your cover letter should provide some reference to your ability to work well with others and the value you place on contributing to the success of an organization. Referring to a recent learning experience such as a relevant course or seminar is helpful. (See Appendix F for a sample cover letter.) Second, make sure your references underscore your positive attitude, loyalty, communication skills, motivational skills, and good work habits. Be sure your references mention your interest in continuous learning for self-improvement. When networking, always exhibit positive work behaviors. Friends and acquaintances will often have an opportunity to put in a good word about you even though they were not listed as formal references. Third, insert frequent references to your good work behaviors throughout the application. An emphasis on adaptability, leadership, teamwork, and productivity is always wise.

During the interview process, you can emphasize your good work behaviors in several ways. Generally, the interviewer will begin by telling you about the company. This is your chance to pick up cues about the behaviors the company most values. This breaking-the-ice period is usually followed by a request for you to tell about your work history. Here is your opportunity to emphasize past successes, being careful to weave in your strong work behaviors. Inevitably, the interviewer will ask you to describe your strengths and weaknesses. This is when you relate your excitement about learning new skills and contributing to the company's success. When you reveal your weaknesses (we all have them), follow up by indicating that you see each weakness as just another learning challenge and that you are currently working on it. The weakness could be in the academic, technical, or behavioral (social) arena.

Assessing and Addressing
Your Basic Deficiencies

Employers are interested in things you know, can do, and feel. They know that no one person excels in everything, and everyone can improve academically, technically, and attitudinally. They respect job applicants who have assessed their deficiencies and are doing something to correct the deficiencies. If an employer perceives that you have a positive attitude, she will admire you and be more likely to employ you.

I recently interviewed the perfect worker. The gentleman spent so much time telling me how wonderful he was, he talked himself out of contention for the job.

People who think they are perfect have at least two major problems: (1) they will lie to you, and (2) they will lie to themselves.

Once you have decided on your long-range career goal and have developed a plan to reach it, discovering your academic and technical deficiencies is easy. Simply match the academic, technical, and physical skills requirements of the career goal (or immediate job) to skills and abilities you already possess. Most public libraries and all college libraries will be able to help you with this task. The United States Department of Labor has numerous publications such as the *Dictionary of Occupational Titles* and the *Occupational Outlook Handbook* that will be useful in this exercise. (Appendix G provides some activities in this regard.)

Discovering social or attitudinal deficiencies is more difficult because we are reluctant to tell others about our shortcomings, and most of us are protective of things that affect our self-esteem. An honest review of your social behavior and personal attitudes can be accomplished by conducting an assessment. You ask (or have someone else ask) your former supervisors, peers, and subordinates to evaluate your team-building, team-playing, communication, and work ethic skills. Most outplacement firms and many employment agencies can do this for you for a fee. Further, several personality assessment instruments are available at your local college, university, or career center. These personality profiles can be very useful in identifying behaviors that come naturally and ones that you'll have to work on. A review of past performance evaluations will often provide the information you need to objectively assess your behavioral deficiencies. Sometimes a candid visit with a good friend can be revealing.

In any case, wise job applicants will seek to discover their deficiencies and resolve to correct them through a personal development plan that may include college courses, professional seminars and training, apprenticeship training, and a conscious effort to change work behaviors. You need to identify your deficiencies and work hard to eliminate them, but do not despair about them. You can accomplish almost anything if your desire is strong enough.

Many famous people have overcome serious deficiencies to be among the best in their career field. Winston Churchill held the lowest academic rank in his elementary school. General George Patton was dyslexic and flunked mathematics at the U.S. Military Academy. Remember Helen Keller? You get the point.

One final note. Many companies provide learning opportunities for their employees. Some, like the McDonnell Douglas Corporation, have developed "learn to earn" programs where employee paychecks are increased in proportion to increased learning. You will do well to ask an interviewer if such learning opportunities are available with the organization. When a prospective employer understands you are interested in self-improvement through staff development opportunities, you'll have one more credit on the right side of the ledger.

Conclusion

Applying the active learner law is essential for seeking and keeping a job in today's changing workplace. Serious job seekers must be willing and eager to correct skills deficiencies in the academic, technical, and behavioral dimensions. Your ability to communicate to prospective employers that you are aware of your strengths and weaknesses and that you constantly work toward improvement is critical during the initial job interview. The goal of this tenth law for getting a job is to convince the prospective employer that you are able to learn new skills and perform in new ways, and that you always have the company's interest at heart.

Practical Advice

Discovering new knowledge, new technical skills, and better workplace behaviors is an exciting part of life. As you work your way through this process of self-improvement to optimize your job opportunities, remember that learning is truly lifelong. The very business of life should include constant growth academically, technically, and attitudinally.

POINTS TO PONDER

1. Learn to earn.
2. Keep your skills current.
3. Demonstrate your skills.
4. Assess and address your deficiencies.

FROM THIS DAY FORWARD

1. I will actively engage in professional development activities that will help me reach my career goal.

2. _____.

3. _____.

4. _____.

CHAPTER 11

HOW TO
GAIN SATS

Few things are impossible to diligence and skill.

—Samuel Johnson

THE ELEVENTH LAW FOR GETTING A GOOD JOB IS HAVING THE PROPER ACADEMIC AND TECHNICAL SKILLS!

You can verify this law by reviewing your past experience with job hunting. In most instances, you were required to meet some minimum educational and/or technical skill levels before being qualified for the job; that is, you had to have "specific academic and technical skills" (SATS). If you are looking for your first job, you can verify this law by looking at the help wanted ads in your newspaper or in a trade-specific journal that lists job openings. Inevitably, all meaningful jobs require a minimum educational level, and most include specific technical skills.

According to the U.S. Department of Labor (1995), the earning power of high-school dropouts is 20 percent less than that of high-school graduates. In 1992, a male college graduate outearned the high-school graduate by 83 percent. Further, job losses for unskilled workers are nearly four times the job losses for college graduates. Certainly not all good jobs require a college degree, but there is a clear statistical advantage for those who increase their academic and technical skills.

It will be prudent for you to consider the usual minimum academic and technical skills required for the job you have targeted. Reading the requirements of job postings in newspapers, journals, and computer networks will give you a representative idea of what academic and technical skills or degrees and certificates you will need to compete for the job you want. As mentioned in chapter 10, other sources of information for this research include the United States Department of Labor publications *Dictionary of Occupational Titles* and *Occupational Outlook Handbook*. These publications should be available at any community or college library. In any event, you will not even be considered if you do not meet these minimum requirements. Human resource personnel make the first cut of applicants by looking at which ones meet the minimum job requirements.

Just how do you prove that you meet the minimums? Most people list their highest academic year or degree earned in addition to any formal training certificates. Unfortunately, most people fail to provide a thorough listing of their academic and technical skills. By thoroughly examining your specific academic and technical skills and listing them convincingly on the job application or in the cover letter, you will reap the benefits of this essential law.

Identifying Your Academic and Technical Assets

You can accomplish a detailed review of your academic and technical skills with just a little effort, and this effort will increase your job opportunities. Remember, your cover letter, resume, and application are the only things that represent you during the screening process. If you do not make it through the screening and get an invitation for an interview, you are wasting your time. Therefore, your cover letter, resume, and application must be professional and thorough in every respect. More important, your goal should be to convince the screeners that you exceed the minimum academic and technical requirements. For example, if the job calls for a high school diploma, you should list it and add anything and everything of significance that demonstrates you exceed the high school diploma. Prior experience is important, also, but that is the subject of chapter 12.

To identify your academic and technical skills, make a list of the following topics:

- Formal education and training
- Informal education and training
- Workplace training
- Hobby and volunteer service skills

Under each category, list things related to your overall academic and technical skills expertise. You will be surprised how knowledgeable and skilled you really are. In the formal education and training category, you should list the highest level of school or college you have achieved thus far. You should also list any vocational or technical certificates or training you have earned through high school, trade school, college, or the military. Also, list your military occupational specialty; this information is important to a screener of applications. If you have a college degree, list your major and minor areas of study. The more information you give, the easier it is for an application screener to get a thorough profile of you. Keep your application succinct but informative. ?

Informal education and training should include any major professional development activities you have experienced on your own, through your church, Scouts, or any other non-work-related organization. Seminars on time management, personal management, or interpersonal communications would be of interest to the application reviewer. First aid, emergency medical technician (EMT), and cardiopulmonary resuscitation skills indicate your interest in others and underscore that you value continuous learning.

Sometimes it is not so much the specific skill that impresses the application reviewer, but the fact that the person has experienced something in common with you. It is human nature for one EMT-certified person, for example, to favor another EMT-certified person when all other qualifications between applicants are equal.

As a self-supporting college student, I was once desperate for a full-time job. A fraternity brother was finishing his degree and leaving his job at a local television station, and he encouraged me to apply. I had absolutely no experience in the field, and I was somewhat intimidated by the prospect of working there. Nonetheless, I applied for the job, and I got it largely because my two interviewers liked me. One of them had belonged to the same fraternity when he was in college, and the other was very supportive of the Boy Scouts of America. I am an Eagle Scout. Both men knew of the character, leadership, and citizenship skills that were provided through our common experiences, and that gave them enough confidence to hire me and train me with the specific skills needed on the job.

Professional development experiences at the workplace are often the most relevant to the new position being sought. Think back through your work history, and list things you learned on the job, either through company-sponsored training or through workplace experience. Do not assume that the application reviewer automatically knows the set of skills you learned from reading your prior job titles. The skills associated with job titles vary a great deal from organization to organization. Either list a brief description of these work-related skills in the work history section of the application, or list them under the education and skills section. For instance, perhaps you were a machinist. Does this mean that you know how to program computer-controlled lathes and milling machines or that you operated these machines? As a graphic artist, are you skilled in computer-aided design software, and have you developed any software of your own? As an accountant, did you learn to write auditing or operational manuals? Did you receive training in customer relations, teamwork, occupational health and safety administration, or aid for disabled Americans? The specifics of meaningful skills in addition to your prior job titles are important.

Finally, job application screeners are interested in your hobbies and non-work-related interests because they paint a more comprehensive profile of who you are. These avocational activities are also a source of specific academic and technical training that most people overlook when completing job applications. Some of your pastime or volunteer activities may give you the edge in the screening process. Obviously, a listing of trivial skills is unwise, but I know of many self-taught computer graphics experts who expanded their job prospects because they knew how to lay out and produce newsletters. Others increase their value to potential employers because they have published newspaper columns or magazine articles. Your volunteer service as a fund-raiser, for example, will be of particular interest to any potential employer. Employers are always interested in people who are committed to helping others, but they may be particularly impressed that you know how to raise money.

Hobbies and volunteer service activities often lead transitional workers into new and more rewarding careers, like the physician in New York City who grew his bread-baking interest into a thriving New England enterprise. One of the largest tea manufacturers in the world, Celestial Seasonings, began with the founder's hobby of collecting herbs and spices from the Colorado mountains. Remember Colonel Sanders? He turned his fried chicken recipe into one of the most prosperous franchises in the world. I know of many people who moved into professional development positions and economic development positions resulting from their volunteering efforts in fund-raising and company relocation.

From personal experience, I can tell you that employers and job application screeners actively look for ways to screen out applicants so they can get to a manageable number of people to interview, usually three to six for each position. The first thing these screeners look for is the minimum educational and training levels required for the job. Next, they look for the required experience minimum. Then they determine which applicants have the highest academic and technical skills and the most experience to help them select finalists to be seriously considered for an interview. I have never discarded an application for being too thorough, but I have pitched hundreds because they did not provide enough information to pique my interest. If you ignore the SATS law, your transition period between jobs will be painfully long.

Confronting Your Academic and Technical Limitations

To get a job with a decent wage and growth potential, you must have mastered the basic skills of reading, writing, and mathematics at the tenth-grade level or higher (most daily newspapers have a ninth-grade readability level or lower). A high school diploma or equivalency is essential. You must also be proficient in the new basic skills that include information-gathering skills, problem-solving skills, the ability to communicate and work well with others, and computer keyboard skills. Many companies now require applicants to prepare their job applications by computer, thereby demonstrating their keyboard competence. If you are deficient in any of these areas, I implore you to take a positive step toward a better future by enrolling at your local community or technical college. If you get the proper skills, you will find a good job. A recent national workforce development survey of more than twenty-five hundred American businesses verified that 75 percent of the businesses need their workers to gain enhanced skills. The National Association of Business

Economists recently reported that 47 percent of American companies are having trouble finding skilled workers.

I can provide hundreds of personal examples of how adults with poor basic skills and low self-esteem have overcome their deficiencies and are now enjoying personal, career, and financial success. Let me tell you about one woman who was a single parent with three children and was living in a homeless shelter when she decided to change her life. With help from our community college and social services, she succeeded in getting a high school equivalency degree, scored a straight A average in her pre-nursing courses, and earned her registered nursing license in three years. She now holds a good job, supports herself and her family, and fully recognizes that people can improve themselves academically if they so desire. One of the most courageous people I have ever met was an illiterate sixty-four-year-old African-American man whose goal was to be able to read and write. After three months of literacy training and with tears of pride streaming down his face, he told me he had just written notes on every Christmas card to his family and friends. Do not be afraid to learn; be afraid not to.

Do not worry about the cost if you have a serious cash flow problem. Your local social services department, one-stop career center, or Work First program should be able to help. Telephone your county or parish department of social services, and they can steer you in the right direction. Also, the college you choose to attend will have admission counselors who can acquaint you with financial aid and scholarship opportunities. And do not worry about how long you have been out of school. These colleges are full of students in their forties, fifties, and sixties!

Without these skills, your chances for landing an ideal job are minimal. Even if you manage to get a good job, you probably will not keep it long if you are deficient in the basic academic skills. Learning has become a lifelong process for today's workers, and all future learning depends on your mastery of these basic skills.

Conclusion

Knowing the specific academic and technical skills needed for your ideal job is essential. If you do not possess or fail to represent these specific skills on your job application, you will remain a worker in transition indefinitely. Identify job-relevant academic and technical skills through an assessment of your formal, informal, workplace, and hobbies-volunteer services training and experiences. Honestly confronting your academic and technical limitations is necessary if you hope to take full advantage of the SATS law.

Practical Advice

Matching your specific academic and technical skills to ones required for a position requires serious attention. First, your cover letter, resume, and application should make it apparent that you not only meet, but exceed, the minimum educational and technical skills required for the job. Second, if you know you have academic limitations related to the occupational position you desire, do whatever it takes to eliminate them or risk remaining underemployed or worse.

POINTS TO PONDER

1. Know your academic and technical capabilities.
2. Record your academic and technical strengths on application materials.
3. Deal with your limitations positively.

FROM THIS DAY FORWARD

1. I will use my academic and technical skills abundantly and work to improve them continuously.

2. _____.

3. _____.

4. _____.

CHAPTER 12

BEEN THERE, DONE THAT

All experience is an arch to build upon.
—Henry Brooks Adams

THE TWELFTH LAW FOR GETTING A JOB IS EMPHASIZING YOUR PRIOR EXPERIENCE!

Many jobs require prior experience as a minimum job qualification. This is entirely within the rights of the employer. Usually, a prior experience requirement is necessary because of some productivity or safety issue. Whatever the case, you must resolve to get the experience needed before making applications for jobs with required prior experience. If you lack the experience needed for a job, do not waste your time or the employer's time by applying. Even if you bluff your way into the position, your ruse will likely be discovered, and your reputation will be tarnished.

You can verify the truth of this law by asking yourself the following questions:

- Would I employ an inexperienced house painter?
- Would I rather have operating on me an experienced or an inexperienced surgeon?
- If I was responsible for managing a construction crew, would I prefer that they be experienced?

Making the Most of Your Experiences

The issue of prior experience is fundamental to most jobs. In practice, most jobs list minimum education and experience requirements that applicants must meet before being considered for the job. But many people ignore these minimum required qualifications and apply anyway. My human resource people tell me that a full 50 percent of applicants for professional positions do not meet the minimums and are automatically discarded. First, they could not handle the job duties, and second, a qualified applicant would have an excellent court case if an unqualified applicant got the job. The point? Do not waste your time or the application screener's time by applying for a job without meeting the minimum requirements.

I know, it is the classic chicken or egg dilemma. If everyone requires prior experience, how can anyone get the first job? Either seek an entry-level position, or determine how to generate experience through some other avenue such as student internships, volunteer service, or a part-time position.

The good news is that you may have experience that qualifies you for more jobs than you suspect. More important, a thorough survey of your work and work-related experience will help you demonstrate experience beyond the minimum job requirements. If you identify a job that fits within your career goal, look carefully at the minimum academic and technical requirements to be sure you meet or exceed them. Next, look at the minimum experience requirements and assess your experience in the area. Begin by listing all direct work-related experience whether it was from a full- or part-time job. Then consider all other relevant experience. For instance, any exposure in the retail market or work with people may qualify as experience in sales and customer relations. The six months you worked in a fast-food restaurant, the time you sold products door-to-door, and even your paper route can apply. At the very least, you could mention your experiences to demonstrate your versatility in sales and customer relations. If you are applying for a job in the health professions, your Red Cross CPR certification, your Scout merit badge, and your volunteer work at the hospital add to your credibility and may be considered equivalent to on-the-job experience. The secret to the experience law, however, is to use the extra experiences to help you exceed the minimum requirements and to demonstrate your versatility.

One of the best methods for gaining the experience needed for a better job is to leverage your opportunities through volunteer service or to exhibit a desire to improve within your current workplace. Several years ago, while I was president of a college in Colorado, a middle-aged instructor told me he had entered the education field after working for many years in industry. He was interested in being reassigned to industrial recruitment and customized training for business and industry. I explained that he would need some specific experiences in those areas before he could be considered for such a position and that no jobs were currently open. He quickly volunteered his services in anything related to this area of the college's activities and requested the opportunity to sit in on one of our company training negotiations. My people were so impressed with his ability to strike a rapport with industrial leaders, he was soon invited to go on an industrial recruitment venture. Within a year, our director of industrial recruitment and customized training took a job out of state and guess who was promoted? Today, this person is the chief operating officer for a college campus of his own.

When you list your prior experience, whether in a cover letter, on a resume, or on a job application, do not exaggerate or stretch the truth. Once a potential employer even suspects that you are less than completely honest, you will be dropped from consideration. I once interviewed a well-groomed, articulate woman for a highly responsible position. The minimum experience required for the job included five years as an administrative assistant to a chief operating officer. Her application indicated that she had such experience. During the first three minutes of the interview, I discovered that she had been only a clerk to a chief operating officer. End of interview.

During the job application process, it is appropriate to mention your indirect experience as a team member or as a participant in a work activity as long as you do not present it as if you directed the project. Employers are interested in people who have high integrity and the ability to work with others. Somewhere in your application materials and especially in the interview, you should communicate your contribution that added real value to former employers or organizations. If you worked on a project that saved your former company money and time, be sure the prospective employer knows it. If you received a merit raise or a bonus for service beyond usual expectations, be sure to mention that, also. Communicate anything that will help the applications screener or the interviewer develop a more comprehensive profile of you as an exceptional employee.

The potential employer needs to understand your knowledge base in terms of workplace needs. What valuable work skills have you learned on the job or through your hobbies and volunteer service? Have you learned to become a good communicator, a persuader, a team player, or a leader? (Appendix H provides an exercise that can be helpful in this discovery process.) The point here is to learn to describe yourself in language that potential employers understand and consider relevant to their needs. As an employer, I listen for self-descriptors such as "enthusiastic," "committed," and "customer focused" when I talk with a job applicant. To describe yourself as "having five years of experience in sales" is one thing. It is much more meaningful to the employer, however, if you describe yourself as "a creative, loyal, and energetic professional with five great years of experience in direct sales."

Coping with Rejection

Inevitably, we all experience failure in the job-hunting process. Rejection from a job you really want and need is always difficult. However, do not take it personally. Many of the decision-making variables are completely out of your hands. Besides, a better opportunity usually appears later on.

Most people can relate personal examples of a failure producing greater success. I once applied for a college presidency because a former colleague encouraged me to do so and because we were interested in returning to Texas where many family members lived. The move would have been lateral in nature, but I thought it offered some new career opportunities. I was selected as a finalist and my interview went so well, the governing board chair asked if I would accept the position. I replied that I would, but he had one more candidate to interview and, in fairness to the college and the other candidate, he should hold the last interview. Much to my astonishment, the board hired the last candidate without a word of explanation to me. My wife and I were crushed emotionally. I learned two good lessons from that event: (1) never delay accepting a job if you want it, and (2) most things happen for good. Less than six months later I was recruited to be the president of one of the largest and most respected colleges in the country!

Just meeting the qualifications of a job does not entitle you to the job. Over the years I have received scores of letters, phone calls, threats, and even civil rights complaints from people who thought they were discriminated against because they met the minimum requirements for a job but did not get it. My advice is to avoid the show of anger. You will burn a bridge unnecessarily, and you will develop a reputation as a person with an entitlement attitude. The Constitution of this country does not guarantee anyone a job. We have to earn jobs or create jobs for ourselves. By following the twelve essential laws for getting a job, you will dramatically increase your chances for getting the job you want in a timely fashion.

Experience Examples

Your primary objective with the experience law is to translate your prior experience into a better job!

Thousands of people have done this and are doing this every day. Dwight D. Eisenhower translated his stellar military career into becoming president of the country. Frank Sinatra translated a successful singing experience into an acting career. John Madden leveraged his football career into a coaching career, and his coaching career paved the way to a network television sports announcing career. You can capitalize on this stair-step career movement by assessing your work-related experience and translating it to meet the needs of a new employer. Continuous self-improvement and career improvement complement each other. As a worker in transition, you will do well to emphasize your prior experience as a major asset for opening the doors to new career opportunities.

Conclusion

Getting a new job involves assessing all your assets, including what you know, believe, and can do. The experience law relates to all three of these basic dimensions. The closer you can relate your work and work-related experiences to the needs of a potential employer, the more likely you will get an interview and eventually the job. Do not bother wasting time applying for jobs where your experience does not meet the required minimums. When you are qualified for a job, do not neglect to list indirect work-related experience in the applications material. Flaunt your experience in a descriptive manner that relates to the workplace needs of employers. Demonstrating a positive attitude along with your experiences, of course, is essential.

Practical Advice

As you assess your direct and indirect work experiences, emphasize what you can do for the prospective employer, not just what you did for another employer. Remember that no one is entitled to a job. We earn jobs by selling our skills and abilities to others, or we create jobs for ourselves. Use all of your prior experience to land a better job. After gaining experience in that job, use it to propel yourself into a promotion or to yet a better job with another organization. You are an enterprise, and you will always be in a state of becoming; that is, you should always be a worker in transition, looking for new opportunities to advance your career. That is what all committed career seekers should be about. There is no finish line. That is the exciting part about working now and into the twenty-first century!

POINTS TO PONDER

1. Assess your direct and related work experiences.
2. Learn to emphasize your experiences in the application.
3. Promote your experiences in workplace language.
4. Take advantage of opportunities for new work-related experiences.

FROM THIS DAY FORWARD

1. I will promote my life and work experiences during job interviews.

2. _____.

3. _____.

4. _____.

CONCLUSION

Transitioning to new jobs has become commonplace in the United States. People who recognize that they are enterprises, fully capable of setting goals, solving problems, adapting to change, and achieving career success will survive handily. People who desperately seek job security and believe they are entitled to a good job with high wages will be unhappy and generally unsuccessful in their careers.

Fortunately, by applying the twelve essential laws for getting a job, you can expect to be successful at securing new jobs and achieving promotions throughout your lifetime. By reading, understanding, and applying the principles of this book, you have every reason to feel secure with yourself and your ability to get good jobs. The only true job security rests with your belief in yourself, a clear job or career goal, and your ability to apply these twelve laws. Once you recognize the truth of this matter, you will be free from the gripping fear of losing a job or applying for a new one. You will also cease being emotionally dependent on your employer or on a particular job. You will experience a freedom from fear and a release from whatever binds you to an unemployment or underemployment condition.

Establishing your career goal, developing a consistently positive attitude, obtaining the right job skills, and having faith in God and yourself will sustain you through the tough times and ultimately propel you into career success. You can begin now to face your next job or promotion acquisition with confidence. You obviously have the personal motivation to excel at the workplace, or you would not have read this entire book in the first place. You can also have confidence in the fact that you have read the right book, know the universal secrets to getting a job, and now have the opportunity to put your knowledge to work for you. You have the right stuff.

Good hunting!

APPENDIX A

TASK-TEAM ANALYSIS

Check sentences that best describe your preferences.

When working, I like to . . .

- ___ 1. Complete job assignments on time.
- ___ 2. Lead a team of coworkers.
- ___ 3. Produce quality work on my own.
- ___ 4. Participate in group assignments.
- ___ 5. Manage my time efficiently.
- ___ 6. Give directions.
- ___ 7. Achieve group consensus.
- ___ 8. Conceive, develop, and implement my ideas.
- ___ 9. Make sure the job is done with precision.
- ___ 10. See others do well at their jobs.
- ___ 11. Be part of a team.
- ___ 12. Brainstorm with others to reach solutions.

Add all checks for sentences numbered 1, 3, 5, 6, 8, 9. This is your "Task" score. Add all checks for sentences numbered 2, 4, 7, 10, 11, 12. This is your "Team" score.

Employers most appreciate employees who have both high "Task" and high "Team" scores. If you have three or fewer checked sentences in either the

"Task" or the "Team" category, you should concentrate on improving your respective low "Task" or "Team" orientation. Employers most desire a proper balance between the two categories.

CAREER ASSESSMENT PROCESS

To determine your basic interests and values, do the following exercises in private. (There are no right or wrong answers.)

Interests

List those activities and hobbies that make you the happiest:

_____   _____
_____   _____
_____   _____
_____   _____

List the names of persons whom you most admire:

_____   _____
_____   _____
_____   _____
_____   _____

Values

Briefly describe what you most admire about each person listed:

_____   _____

_____   _____

_____   _____

_____   _____

Now review the exercises and circle the things that most interest you and that you most value. These circled items represent your highest interests and values. As you begin to focus on a job group, keep these interests and values in mind. By choosing a job that features these same attributes, you will definitely be happier and more productive at work.

List six personal accomplishments achieved alone or with a group (they can be things you're proud of from your childhood to today):

1. _____

2. _____

3. _____

4. _____

5. _____

6. _____

Now review these accomplishments and identify the particular part of each accomplishment that you most enjoyed. Was it because you achieved a goal by yourself, because you helped others, or because you exhibited leadership skills? This self-review should also reveal some of your true interests and values.

The next interest and values exercise was developed by the U.S. Department of Labor Employment and Training Division and is published in the *Guide for Occupational Exploration*. This guide provides an inventory of twelve interest areas and twenty-seven values areas. First, place a check mark next to each interest and values area that indicates the kind of work you would like to do. Then go back and add a second check mark next to the three interests and three values that most appeal to you.

Interest Inventory

___ 1. Artistic: An interest in creative expression of feelings or ideas.

___ 2. Scientific: An interest in discovering, collecting, and analyzing information about the natural world, and in applying scientific research findings to problems in medicine, the life sciences, and the natural sciences.

___ 3. Plants and animals: An interest in working with plants and animals, usually outdoors.

___ 4. Protective: An interest in using authority to protect people and property.

___ 5. Mechanical: An interest in applying mechanical principles to practical situations by use of machines or hand tools.

___ 6. Industrial: An interest in repetitive, concrete, organized activities done in a factory setting.

___ 7. Business detail: An interest in organized, clearly defined activities requiring accuracy and attention to details, primarily in an office setting.

___ 8. Selling: An interest in bringing others to a particular point of view by personal persuasion, using sales and promotion techniques.

___ 9. Accommodating: An interest in catering to the wishes and needs of others, usually on a one-to-one basis.

___ 10. Humanitarian: An interest in helping others with their mental, spiritual, social, physical, or vocational needs.

___ 11. Leading and influencing: An interest in leading and influencing others by using high-level verbal or numerical abilities.

___ 12. Physical performing: An interest in physical activities performed before an audience.

Values Inventory

___ 1. Adventure: Working in a job that requires taking risks.

___ 2. Authority: Working in a job in which you use your position to control others.

___ 3. Competition: Working in a job in which you compete with others.

___ 4. Creativity and self-expression: Working in a job in which you use your imagination to do or say something.

___ 5. Flexible work schedule: Working in a job in which you choose your hours of work.

___ 6. Helping others: Working in a job in which you provide direct services to persons with problems.

___ 7. High salary: Working in a job where many workers earn a large amount of money.

___ 8. Independence: Working in a job in which you decide for yourself what work to do and how to do it.

___ 9. Influencing others: Working in a job in which you influence the opinions or decisions of others.

___ 10. Intellectual stimulation: Working in a job that requires a considerable amount of thought and reasoning.

___ 11. Leadership: Working in a job in which you direct, manage, or supervise the activities of others.

___ 12. Outside work: Working out-of-doors.

___ 13. Persuading: Working in a job in which you personally convince others to take certain action.

___ 14. Physical work: Working in a job that requires substantial physical activity.

___ 15. Prestige: Working in a job that gives you status and respect in the community.

___ 16. Public attention: Working in a job in which you attract immediate notice because of appearance or activity.

___ 17. Public contact: Working in a job in which you have day-to-day dealings with the public.

___ 18. Recognition: Working in a job where you gain public notice.

___ 19. Research work: Working in a job in which you search for and discover new facts and develop ways to apply them.

___ 20. Routine work: Working in a job in which you follow established procedures requiring little change.

___ 21. Seasonal work: Working in a job in which you are employed only at certain times of the year.

___ 22. Travel: Working in a job in which you take frequent trips.

___ 23. Variety: Working in a job in which your duties change frequently.

___ 24. Work with children: Working in a job in which you teach or otherwise care for children.

___ 25. Work with hands: Working in a job in which you use your hands or hand tools.

___ 26. Work with machines or equipment: Working in a job in which you use machines or equipment.

___ 27. Work with numbers: Working in a job in which you use mathematics or statistics.

Guide for Occupational Exploration, second edition, edited by Thomas F. Harrington and Arthur J. O'Shea, © 1984 American Guidance Service, Inc., 4201 Woodland Road, Circle Pines, Minnesota 55014-1796. All rights reserved. Reproduced with permission of the publisher. Out of print.

What do you really want to do with your life? You need to answer this fundamental question before you settle on a career or job goal because you will spend the major part of your life at the workplace. If you are not happy at your job, you will never excel at it, and you will have wasted a good portion of your life. These next exercises are designed to help you focus on your immediate job objective and long-term career goal. This job most closely allows you to accomplish your life's ambition. As you complete these exercises, remember that now is the time of truth. You are doing this for yourself only, and there are no wrong answers.

Pretend that your life ends this very moment. Now list five adjectives your friends would most likely use to describe your personality:

He (or she) was   1. _____

                      2. _____

                      3. _____

                      4. _____

                      5. _____

Next, list the five accomplishments your obituary would likely report:

He (or she)   1. _____

                      2. _____

                      3. _____

                      4. _____

                      5. _____

Now, review your responses. These exercises are intended to help you step away from yourself for a moment and concentrate on who you are and what you have accomplished to this point in your life. If you are unhappy with who you have been and what you have accomplished, you can set higher goals to accomplish. Go back to the exercises, print in bold letters the different or additional adjectives you would like to describe you. In the following spaces, write a different job objective or career goal that you would like to accomplish in your lifetime.

Job objective: Within _____ weeks, I will be

employed _____

_____.

Career goal: I intend to _____

_____.

These descriptors and life goals should become your primary tools for selecting the immediate job objective and long-term career goal. Of course, the simple task of writing these desires on paper is a far cry from achieving them. Behavioral research indicates that you will become and accomplish what you most desire and believe. Therefore, no matter how strange, bold, or different your new pursuits are, you will be successful if you truly want them, believe you can achieve them, and have a good plan to follow.

SAMPLE CONTACT LIST FORMAT

Begin developing your contact lists as soon as possible. Companies do not hire people; people hire people. You need to write several lists of acquaintances who could help you in any manner related to your job search. Some possible general lists should include old friends, new friends, relatives, and referrals.

An effective example of a contact list looks like this:

Old Friends

From Work	Contact Date & Notes	Follow-Up & Notes
_____	_____	_____
_____	_____	_____
_____	_____	_____

From Church	Contact Date & Notes	Follow-Up & Notes
_____	_____	_____
_____	_____	_____
_____	_____	_____

From School Contact Date & Notes Follow-Up & Notes

_____ _____ _____
_____ _____ _____
_____ _____ _____

From Social or Civic Clubs Contact Date & Notes Follow-Up & Notes

_____ _____ _____
_____ _____ _____
_____ _____ _____

From Volunteer Projects Contact Date & Notes Follow-Up & Notes

_____ _____ _____
_____ _____ _____
_____ _____ _____

From Political Activities Contact Date & Notes Follow-Up & Notes

_____ _____ _____
_____ _____ _____
_____ _____ _____

XYZ CORPORATION— SAMPLE EMPLOYER CONTACT FORMAT

Date of first contact: _____

Referred by (person, agency, newspaper ad, etc.): _____

Company summary: _____

Key contact(s): _____

Name (usually the human resources

   director): _____

Phone no: _____

Address: _____

_____

_____

First contact information:

   Summary of contact: Need to follow up? _____

                                     Thank-you note? _____

Second contact information:

   Summary of contact: Need to follow up? _____

                                     Thank-you note? _____

CAREER GOAL EXERCISE

The following exercise is the most important in the entire book. Your responses to these five statements will form the core of your job search plan and will prepare you with the confidence that comes from knowing yourself and what you can do for an employer. Use only one sentence for each statement.

1. State your immediate job objective.

   _____

   _____

2. State your career goal (or where you intend to be ten years from now).

   _____

   _____

3. State why the employer should hire you (specify personality traits).

   _____

   _____

4. State your specific credentials for the job.

_____

_____

5. State why you've chosen this career field.

_____

_____

The completion of this exercise will result in a five-sentence biography that you can relate in clear language while networking, talking on the telephone during query calls, filling out a job application, or responding to an interviewer. You could even have this snappy biography printed on your business cards or on the flap of your personalized thank-you notes!

SAMPLE COVER LETTER

Dear _____ :

Enclosed are application materials for the position titled "_____." My goal is to provide a significant contribution by working collaboratively to help *(company name)* reach its vision. I am confident that my communication skills, employer loyalty, and work-specific skills match those needed to excel in this position.

I urge you to read my reference letters and call my current/previous employers. You will find that my enthusiasm, leadership skills, and problem-solving abilities are outstanding. Thank you for considering me for an interview.

I will telephone your office in a few days to see if you would like additional information or have any questions.

Cordially,

Name

Address

ACADEMIC-TECHNICAL SKILLS ASSESSMENT

Complete the following exercises to determine your strengths and weaknesses in the knowledge area.

List all major education and training learned through an educational institution:

High School	College	Military
_____	_____	_____
_____	_____	_____
_____	_____	_____
_____	_____	_____

List all major education and training learned through a job, through a hobby, or through volunteer service:

On-the-Job Training	Hobby or Volunteer Service
_____	_____
_____	_____
_____	_____
_____	_____

Now match your career goals or immediate job objective knowledge and skills requirements to your knowledge and skills listed in this assessment activity. Correct any apparent deficiencies.

DISCOVER YOUR PERSONALITY TRAITS

Most likely, you easily listed academic subject areas in the Appendix G exercises but found it more difficult to list what you have learned on the job and through hobbies or volunteer service. The purpose of this exercise is to help you realize that subject areas by themselves are not very meaningful to you in the job search process. You and the potential employer need to understand your knowledge base in terms of workplace needs. The following list of social and workplace skills will help to identify your special knowledge or skills in this regard.

Circle the words that best describe your abilities:

Writing	Organizing
Speaking	Arbitrating
Persuading	Motivating
Selling	Conceptualizing
Problem Solving	Detail Oriented
Leading	Socially Sensitive

Creating	Politically Astute
Analyzing	Honest
Managing	Diligent
Coaching	Patient
Cheering	Reliable
Goals Setting	Task Completing
Enthusiastic	Loyal

Once you have completed this exercise, practice describing yourself with the words you have circled. Employers understand these words, and when that important interview arrives, you'll be talking their language! To describe yourself as "holding a bachelor's degree in business" is one thing. It's much more meaningful to the employer, however, if you describe yourself as "a creative, loyal, and energetic professional with a degree in business."

ABOUT THE AUTHOR

Tony Zeiss holds a doctorate in higher education and is a nationally recognized leader in workforce development. His twenty-eight years of experience in higher education have been highlighted by his prominence in economic and workforce development.

He supervised the development of one of the first U.S. Department of Labor approved skills centers, chaired the Colorado State Job Training Coordinating Council, and led two colleges into national prominence through his focus on America's workforce.

He is a prolific writer and speaker whose previous books include *Economic Development: A Viewpoint of Business, Creating a Literate Society* (with a preface by Barbara Bush), *Community College Leadership in the Twenty-First Century,* and *A Mission of America's Community Colleges: Developing the World's Most Skilled and Adaptable Workforce.* He is also a popular consultant and is a professional speaker for the Zig Ziglar Corporation.

Dr. Zeiss is currently president of Central Piedmont Community College, which serves 62,000 students each year in Charlotte, North Carolina, and is chair of the American Association of Community Colleges' National Commission on Workforce and Community Development.